PRAISE FOR *LO*

Do you want to be prepared for your fi⋯
workforce has been through a radical ⋯
every person working today will benefit from the wisdom and insight given
between these covers.

RICHARD GLASS | Director, Career Center, Liberty University

Robert Dickie's newest book, *Love Your Work*, outlines the path and the plans
to help you escape the emotional and financial drain of a job that doesn't meet
your needs or motivate you to achieve your God-given potential. Get it. Read
it. Pivot to the career you were made for!

CHUCK BENTLEY | CEO, Crown Financial Ministries

As a college professor and student advisor, I am always looking for practical
tools that help my students identify and harness their passions, talents, and
God-given abilities. I appreciate the "on the ground" approach in this book
where Robert uses "Pivot Points" to provide straightforward action steps and
experiential learning each step of the way! I will be recommending this book
to my students and colleagues.

BARBARA A. HERTER | Rinker School of Business, Palm Beach Atlantic
University

We millennials often need to be reminded not only *what* to do and *how* to do
it, but *why*. We need to know our work matters. We come alive at the intersection of skill and meaning, and *Love Your Work* shows us how to get there.
This is an extremely insightful guide to help you use your passion to make an
impact on your world.

ALLIE BETH STUCKEY | The Conservative Millennial Blog

A must read for those in career transition or those looking for something
more. The practical resources and actionable tools not only help someone
pivot to a new life-fulfilling career, but also give real-life examples to inspire
and to motivate. Invest in yourself with this great resource.

JEREMIE KUBICEK | CEO of GiANT Worldwide and bestselling author

If you are ready to move from going through the motions to loving your work
and living into your faith, your passion, your gifts and skills, then this is the
book for you. Within these pages Robert Dickie gives you fresh tools to help
you pivot toward a career that both fits you and fits our fast-changing work
landscape. Dive in and discover how you can begin to prepare yourself for the
kind of position where you can thrive.

TOM OGBURN | First Baptist Church Knoxville

There's no denying that life comes at us fast. The same has been the case with the pace at which industries are changing and the nature of work as we've known it has been eroded. Once again, Robert Dickie III has provided us with an invaluable resource to practically navigate those changes. I am confident that many lives will be impacted by the information, wisdom, and tangible resources provided throughout this professional journey in book form. If you're ready for a pivot, there is no time like the present, and this book can serve as your catalyst.

REGGIE LEONARD | Assistant Director for Career Services, University of Virginia

If you have ever got to the point in your career where you have wondered "is this all there is?" or thought "so this is how it ends?", in his latest book *Love Your Work* Robert Dickie makes it clear that it doesn't have to be drudgery and boredom in our careers. Robert shows us how to analyze our current career and if we have to make a "pivot" what steps we should take to increase the odds of making it the right one. Really, this book is a step-by-step how to get the most out of our careers for the glory of God.

TIM MARKS | President, Bonvera

A must read for those in career transition or those looking for something more. Robert Dickie has packed his book with practical resources and actionable tools to help someone pivot to a new fulfilling career. He weaves powerful stories with real-life examples of those who have pivoted to a better career to help those wishing to do the same.

JOEL WIDMER | Founder and CEO, Fluxe Digital Marketing

LOVE YOUR WORK

4 PRACTICAL WAYS
YOU CAN PIVOT
TO YOUR BEST
CAREER

ROBERT DICKIE III

MOODY PUBLISHERS

CHICAGO

650.1
D

© 2017 by
ROBERT DICKIE III

All Scripture quotations, unless otherwise indicated, are taken from the Holy Bible, New International Version®, NIV®. Copyright © 1973, 1978, 1984, 2011 by Biblica, Inc.™ Used by permission of Zondervan. All rights reserved worldwide. www.zondervan.com. The "NIV" and "New International Version" are trademarks registered in the United States Patent and Trademark Office by Biblica, Inc.™

Edited by Elizabeth Cody Newenhuyse
Cover design: Faceout Studio and Erik M. Peterson
Interior design: Smartt Guys design
Author photo: Walid Azami Studio

215:Ill.

ISBN: 978-0-8024-1486-1

We hope you enjoy this book from Moody Publishers. Our goal is to provide high-quality, thought-provoking books and products that connect truth to your real needs and challenges. For more information on other books and products written and produced from a biblical perspective, go to www.moodypublishers.com or write to:

Moody Publishers
820 N. La Salle Boulevard
Chicago, IL 60610

3 5 7 9 10 8 6 4 2

Printed in the United States of America

I DEDICATE THIS BOOK to the Great Recession "refugees" who worked hard, followed instructions, and did everything they were told to do to achieve the American dream. Like me, you just wanted a fulfilling career, to make a difference in the world, to be able to provide for yourself, maybe your family, and help others along the way. You followed the plan, perfectly checking the boxes along the way, only to wake up one morning and realize the path you followed had led to a destination that was less than desirable and left you unsatisfied with your career. Instead of being passionate about what you were doing, maybe you found yourself just getting by. You noticed the world changing around you, and you realized the game plan you had been following left you unprepared for the reality you faced.

But now, instead of waiting for the next surprise around the corner, you are ready to take action. Instead of letting the life slowly get sucked out of you each week, you are ready to "jail-break" your career. Instead of dreading Monday morning, you are ready to create your escape to the job, career, and future you always wanted.

It has been said, "Depression is being trapped in the past. Anxiety is being trapped in the future." I dedicate this book to those who refuse both of those positions and are living in the moment— ready to start a new, exciting journey to the work they love and a career that is meaningful. #RiseUp

CONTENTS

Chapter 1—Here Comes the Tide of Change!   9

Chapter 2—The Power of Restorative Work   27

Chapter 3—The Four Career Quadrants   49

Chapter 4—Knowing Your Transcending Career Skills   73

Chapter 5—Make It Happen   111

Chapter 6—Currents of Growth and Opportunity   133

Chapter 7—Leverage Failure   157

Chapter 8—The Long Gear: Small Steps to Success   175

Notes   205

Resources and Websites   209

Acknowledgments   213

About the Author   215

1

HERE COMES THE TIDE OF CHANGE!

"The man who stands firm to protect sandcastles can never be relied upon; for he has given away his common sense."
WINSTON CHURCHILL

The warm breeze blowing across the sand mingles with the rhythmic sounds of the waves rolling onto the beach to provide the perfect ambient soundscape as I enjoy an indulgent nap while on vacation. Kiawah Island, South Carolina, has become my family's retreat. It is a quiet place to unwind and thaw out from a long winter. No beach trip is complete without sand castles and kites, and my son and daughters love digging in the sand, re-creating the walls, moats, and bridges of Disney fairylands. I'll watch from a distance as the castle gets larger and more intricate, and hours of fun are spent building, playing, and dreaming while their backs are to the sea, temporarily unaware of the approaching tide. Soon the long runs to the water become a few steps, and then the sea is lapping around their feet as they try to build the walls higher and higher to block the tide from washing away their handiwork.

Soon I hear the cries of "Dad, come help us!" as they feverishly dig to save a day's worth of construction. I do what I can, but we all know how this will end. Once again, our valiant efforts to save the castle prove futile, as the sea slowly, without thought or feeling, washes around the walls and over the castle until it is no more.

During our time at Kiawah Island, it has become a daily ritual as we pack up to leave the beach that the children plan where they will build the next day. "Tomorrow let's build it further away from the ocean," says London. "Or maybe we can build deeper moats and higher walls. Dad, will that protect the castle?" asks Amaris. The next morning as we approach the beach, the ocean is far in the distance, beyond a vast blank canvas of clean, untouched white sand. There is no sign of the castle from the day before. Just a perfect beach ready for another day of fun and imagination as we create something new for us to enjoy for a brief moment in time.

A NEW BLANK CANVAS

Just as my children wake to a fresh new beach each morning on Kiawah Island, giving them a blank canvas on which to create and have fun, the tide of economic change is also washing over the landscape, creating a new canvas of opportunity for people ready to try something new. The old economic systems are fading away, and a new global economy is being born that will usher in opportunity and new ways of intentionally engineering our lives and developing our careers. We will have opportunities our parents and grandparents never had, but to survive and thrive amid the tide of change, we will be required to think and plan differently. Our success will depend on it.

To put the changes we face into context, think back to 1908 when Henry Ford introduced the Model T vehicle in North America. The predominant mode of transportation at that time

THE PAST

Great Opportunity

was still horse-drawn carriages. The nation's entire transportation system was built around the horse. Whole industries served this sector—wagon makers, stable hands, even street cleaners to pick up what the horses left behind. As it always happens, most assumed that this way of doing things would continue indefinitely. So the Model T was seen at first as a novelty item. Few felt threatened by it.

Boy, did that change quickly. Just a few short years later the Model T was the top-selling vehicle in the United States. Over 50 percent of all drivers in America learned how to drive on a Model T.[1] Businesses that had been rooted in the old economic paradigm—but quickly pivoted to start supplying this new industry of "horseless carriages"—did very well.

Take Lawrence Fisher. He started a horse-drawn carriage shop in the 1880s in Norwalk, Ohio. By 1905, Lawrence's two sons, Fred and Charles Fisher, seeing the writing on the wall, moved to Detroit to be a part of the new industry being born. In 1908 they started Fisher Body Company; by 1910, they were building the bodies for Cadillac and Buick. By 1913, they were able to produce 100,000 vehicle bodies a year, which increased to over 370,000 by 1916.[2] General Motors bought Fisher Body in 1926, and the brand was a mainstay for General Motors until the late 1990s. The Fisher brothers' ability to see the future and pivot the family business to be able to take advantage of the new developments allowed them to have incredible success. Those who refused to change and were still selling buggy whips in 1920 did not fare well.

We have a similar tectonic shift taking place. We have the same opportunities today that the Fisher brothers observed in 1905. As the world changes, regardless of our age, education, background, skill sets, or experience, we all have the ability to move out of the old economy and pivot into the new. Our view of change is many times based on how it impacts us and how prepared we are. Today, those who are benefiting from change love it. There are many people who are benefiting from increased trade, growth of technology, and new industries that are being born as the old ones die. Those who are not prepared or are being displaced as their industries change or go away, those who face diminishing wages or, worse yet, the loss of a job can, understandably, fear change.

However, nostalgia for the past will not help. We must be prepared as we look to make career pivots to the work we love.

CURRENT REALITY

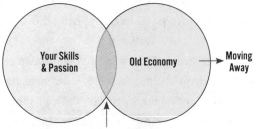

Your Skills & Passion

Old Economy

Moving Away

Shrinking Opportunities and Displacement

And it is never too late! The number of people who are doing this later in their career is growing, as shown by a 2014 study by Encore.org, which reported that more than 4.5 million Americans pivoted mid-career to find a different job.[3] Furthermore, a research study by the American Institute for Economic Research shows that 82 percent of people who pivot to a new career make a successful transition![4] We don't need to fear change. Rather, embracing change is critical for our success.

NEW ECONOMY BEING BORN

THE PIVOT

As the sun slowly descends into the ocean out on the horizon, I love the chatter of my children planning for the next day. "What time should we get to the beach and where should we set up our home base? Where should we start building the next castle and what should we do different?" they ask. There is a joy and excitement in their voices as they plan the adventures of the next day. Taking lessons from the day, they devise new plans to build their castle with different barriers and techniques to protect the walls. These small changes to their plans are very similar to what I have come to learn in the business world as "pivots." It is a common practice to take a business plan or idea and, over time, iterate—tweak the plan, make small changes to the company—as a response to changes in the environment and marketplace. The business world boasts many stories of entrepreneurs who made pivots to their plan on their way to greater and greater success. Fisher Body is one example from a century ago. Twitter offers a great example from today.

Team members created a mechanism known as "twttr" that allowed them to share short messages with each other.

Tech entrepreneur Evan Williams started the first blogging service—known as Blogger—that was sold to Google in 2003. He is credited with coining the term "blog" and starting this new revolution that many have credited for helping transform publishing. Little did he know that his invention would be a wave that would wash away a very big sandcastle in the newspaper business. After leaving Google he started Odeo, a podcasting company that soon was struggling and not having success with its original business plan. Internally, team members had created a micro-blogging mechanism known as "twttr" that allowed them to share short messages up to 140 characters with each other. Evan immediately saw the potential, and as Odeo continued to struggle, he pivoted his business plan to focus all his efforts and energy on what would become Twitter, today one of the Internet's top ten websites in traffic.

"Pivoting" has become a ubiquitous phrase in the technology, start-up, and entrepreneurial world as founders and entrepreneurs will take business plans and over time iterate or "pivot" as the market changes. They are always ready and willing to pivot to success. Pivots are slight changes to a plan that allow the person to leverage skill sets, past knowledge, and experience to do something new. This slight change can help someone move from a career dead end or low-opportunity job to a new industry or market rich with potential. Instead of standing still and letting the world change around them, or, worse yet, quitting, entrepreneurs have learned the art of small micro-adjustments that allow them to continue to move and grow in an ever-changing environment until they find the sweet spot for their company.

Or consider Jeff Bezos. When he launched Amazon as a

book-ordering service, he would fill orders by actually going out to a bookstore and buying the requested title. He would then ship it to the customer. In effect, he was offering delivery service—convenience. Over time he slowly made adjustments and added new features. Bezos did not try to start Amazon as the global giant it has become, offering almost anything you can imagine. He pivoted, and kept pivoting.

To see what happens to companies that do not change and fail to keep up with the marketplace, we can read Jim Collins's bestseller *How the Mighty Fall,* which chronicles the demise of great companies for lack of leadership and innovation. Who would have thought that Kodak, the iconic American company that essentially made it possible for average consumers to take photos of everything from their dogs to the Grand Canyon, would go bankrupt the same year that online upstart Instagram, a service that allows people to share and edit photos, would be valued at over a billion dollars? Companies that don't innovate and stay in touch with new market developments go out of business. The same happens with people if we are not aware and staying current in our careers.

Just as Fisher Body and Twitter in different centuries leveraged pivots for success, we must do the same in our careers today. The new reality makes it extremely important for us to know *why* we need to do this—and *how.*

CHANGE = NEW OPPORTUNITY

We are seeing two major changes—one personal, one global—that will impact everyone. First, normal career path and work engagement have fundamentally shifted and will continue to do so for the next few decades. Second, with the rise of globalization and advancement of technology, whole industries are being revolutionized. Many others are going extinct.

But many of us grew up with a different paradigm for our lives and work. The Industrial Revolution and the rise of large-scale manufacturing at the turn of the twentieth century ushered in an era of big corporations that provided what appeared to be safe and reliable employment, careers that could last up to thirty to forty years at a company—with benefits and guaranteed retirement upon the completion of a career. Our grandparents were able to plan out a lifetime and dream of a retirement in a beachfront community in Florida or desert oasis in Arizona. Those starting their career in whatever field of endeavor could, with a high degree of certainty, bank on the "Forty-Five-Year Plan."

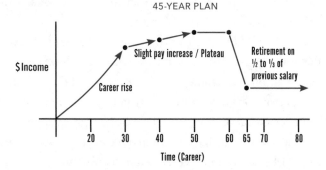

The path to the American dream was to choose a career field early in life, obtain education and skills in our twenties, and slowly but steadily advance until we hit a plateau of earning potential. Then we would continue there for the bulk of our careers with uninterrupted work until retirement where we would retire on a third of our salary with a guaranteed and supposedly safe pension plan. Hello South Florida, here we come!

The safety of this system was no less secure from the tides of time as my children's sand castles on the beach. We started to see fissures in the foundation of this system as big and highly respected companies like Enron and WorldCom went bankrupt in 2001 and

2003, respectively, costing employees their jobs and investors their money. During the economic Great Recession of 2009, many more companies like Bear Stearns and Lehman Brothers collapsed, eliminating millions of safe and secure jobs overnight. Others, such as General Motors and AIG, had to be totally restructured to be saved. Even local governments were not safe from the tides of economic change. Local municipalities like Stockton, California, and Detroit, Michigan, unable to cover their operating costs and debt obligations to include pension plans for local service officials like police, fire, and other government workers, filed for bankruptcy and started to cut and reduce pension plans for retirees. So much for that safe and secure government job and guaranteed retirement plan!

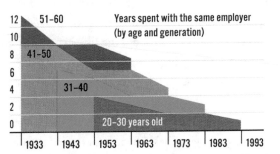

Graph adapted from *Fortune* magazine, "A Millennial's Field Guide to Mastering Your Career" by Clarie Groden, January 1, 2016.

Now, long-term, uninterrupted employment in single industries, followed by a guaranteed safe retirement, is seen as a relic of a generation long past. From millennials to baby boomers, the new norm is short-term employment stints at companies, freelance work on the side, working multiple jobs, gaps in employment as people look for work, and retirement-age employees working longer and even starting "encore careers" that they will enjoy in an exciting new stage of life.

Earl Williams, General Electric's manager of employee benefits, wrote, "Maximizing employee security is a prime company goal."[5] Does that sound strange, compared to how many companies operate today? It should, because that was written in 1962. Reid Hoffman, the founder of LinkedIn.com and coauthor of *The Alliance*, says, contemplating Williams's quote, "In that era, careers were considered nearly as permanent as marriage."[6] Marshall Goldsmith summed up the new reality when he said, "*Fast Company* nailed it in 1998 when it ran a notorious cover story titled 'Free Agent Nation.' It posited the then-radical notion that the organization man was dead, that the best performers in a company were no longer interested in sacrificing their lives for the good of the organization. The smart ones believed that their corporation would drop them in a flash when they no longer met the company's needs, so they in turn were willing to drop the company when it no longer met their needs. Free agent meant that each employee was operating like a small self-contained business rather than a cog in the wheel of a large system."[7]

As the waves of the new global economy washed over the structures of the past, entire industries—automotive, retail, publishing, media, communications, and entertainment, to name a few—underwent far-reaching changes. These changes had dramatic consequences for employees in these companies. Icons of industry that did not quickly adapt to the new era went out of business—Kodak, Blockbuster, TWA, Woolworths. Just a few years later, tech companies like Yahoo that were once the darlings of their industry struggled to remain relevant and solvent as the world changed faster than they could. Think about it: one day you have a job at a company that is at the center of cutting-edge Silicon Valley innovation; the next day its struggle for survival is front-page news across all forms of media, new and old. Eventually it disappears, swallowed up by another company.

Scary? Yes.

But: regardless of what happens to the companies we work for, when we are prepared we realize these changes are opening new opportunities for success. In the military, one of my first commanders taught the young officers never to say, "Boss, we have a problem," but rather to meet every problem with the attitude of "We have an opportunity for success." That has stuck with me throughout my career, and it is especially applicable to how we should view the new global economy. We will all have opportunities to pivot in our careers, and each time we do it will be an opportunity for success!

To further highlight these changes during the last six decades, job creation in the United States averaged from 20–30 percent per decade.

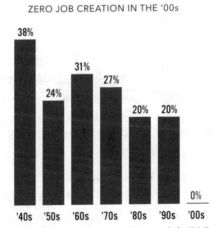

ZERO JOB CREATION IN THE '00s

Graph adapted from *The Washington Post*, "Aughts Were a Lost Decade for U.S. Economy, Workers" by Neil Irwin, January 2, 2010.

From 2000 to 2010, job growth was down 1.9 percent in a stunning reversal from sixty years of growth.[8] As companies struggled in a low-growth market and shifted jobs overseas, workers worldwide caught up in this sea of change were pressed on two sides as globalization rapidly moved jobs and industries overseas to lower-cost environments, and technological advancements automated many jobs that no longer needed manual or human interaction.

Old methods of manufacturing vehicles where plants would have 10,000 workers on production lines were transformed where Lexus factories in Japan could employ 1,000 workers to produce the same number of vehicles and with higher quality. Titans of industry like Chrysler and GM faltered, while disruptive, technology-forward companies like Tesla rose to prominence in their place.

Meanwhile, such occupations as secretaries, file clerks, and bookkeepers disappeared as new technologies supplanted human effort and recession-battered companies sought to cut costs. Those employed in industries ranging from textiles to manufacturing to newspapers were let go, "refugees of the recession," and this phenomenon is far from over.

So . . . what do we do?

Like Evan Williams of Twitter and Fred and Charles Fisher, who pivoted their companies to take advantage of new opportunities, we must pivot in our careers and we must learn how to do it quickly.

THE NEW FRONTIER: AREAS OF MASSIVE GROWTH AND OPPORTUNITY

What, then, are the big, booming industries being created today with exciting opportunities for us to pivot to? Anything in technology has a long runway for the next twenty to thirty years. The chairman of Cisco, John Chambers, speaking to *Fortune* magazine's Global Forum, said experts anticipate there will be 500 billion connected devices by 2025 instead of the 25 billion predicted earlier.[9] The world is changing much faster than anticipated! 3-D printing is radically changing manufacturing. The pharmaceutical industry is growing by leaps and bounds with new advancements. Health care is growing, and in particular home care and services for a large baby boomer population that over the next decade will see 10,000 baby boomers turn sixty-five every day![10] The freelancer economy continues to grow as the nature of work in this country changes, and remote staffing and part-time staffing is a red-hot industry with increasing opportunity. With the spread of connected devices, data proliferation is happening at a rapid pace. Companies have more access to data on

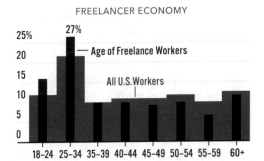

FREELANCER ECONOMY

Graph adapted from *Fortune* magazine, "A Millennial's Field Guide to Mastering Your Career" by Claire Groden, January 1, 2016.

their customers than ever before yet struggle to know how to use it. Data Science is a new career field that did not exist a few short years ago. It is so highly sought after that institutions like the University of Virginia have established brand-new majors to train students in this field of study, and graduates are snatched up instantly upon completion of the program.

Finally, green and renewable energy will continue to impact our global economies for decades to come. Advancements in wind and solar power are changing the way we build homes, cities, and cars of the future. Battery advancement is changing everything from handheld devices to the potential for deep-space exploration, as Space X and Elon Musk have made more advancements for space travel in the past few years than NASA has in the past few decades. Scientists in the middle of 2016 put a specially made 3-D printer on the International Space Station so needed tools and parts could be created in space![11] If you ever looked up to the stars as a child and wondered what it would be like to explore them, our children today are closer than ever before to that opportunity.

So how does this help us? What can we do to take advantage of these great opportunities? What should a high-school student do to pick the right course of study so they are entering an industry and career that is on the upswing with decades of potential, and not an industry fading into the past? How does a mid-career professional who feels disenfranchised in their work make a pivot? Where should they go and how do they make the transition? What should a boomer do for their "next phase"?

If you know someone who is struggling and needs help, this guide will help them. Maybe you know that you need to make a pivot because your company or industry is on the downward trend. Maybe you are just not satisfied with your current job and want to find your passion in life and do something meaningful and with purpose, but are so far down the road that you feel like you missed your opportunity and don't know how to hit the reset button. If you find yourself in these situations, this book will show you how to pivot, to start over, and to find the work you love. Most people don't like change, and many can find it scary, but I hope through this book you will come to better understand what is currently happening and realize you have the greatest opportunity ever to pivot—and do what you always thought you were called to do!

Whether you are a millennial who is expected to have from eight to fourteen different careers or "pivots" in your lifetime, or a baby boomer who thought you would ease into retirement and now realize you need to pivot to a retirement career, you will need to adjust quickly to seize opportunities as the tides alter the landscape around us. Now is not the time for us to be yearning for the days of the past, continuing to sell horse and buggy whips. Author Neil Gaiman said in a commencement address, "The old rules are crumbling and no one knows what the new rules are, so make up your own!"[12] The tides that bring us change also bring us great opportunity to build exciting lives that past generations could only dream about. We just have to seize the opportunity.

> **PIVOT POINTS** Knowledge Is Power

It has been said that knowledge is power, and in today's quickly changing economy that is certainly the case. It is important to have your finger on the pulse of the global economy and especially the technology sector. As we have already discussed, technological advancements are impacting every industry, even ones you wouldn't think would be affected, like fast food. Those who are at the forefront and understand what is going on have a tremendous advantage. It is like being in the stock market with insider information. Don't be the guy walking in the front door of work one morning with the security guard there saying, "Hey, didn't you hear? The company went bankrupt yesterday. It's been all over the news." A day late and dollar short never works well. These free resources have been invaluable to me in my career, and I know they will serve you equally well. They will help you stay in touch with key aspects of the global economy while expanding your knowledge and education.

1. **THE WALL STREET JOURNAL (WSJ.COM)** – Taking twenty minutes a day to read the major headlines will keep you informed on global topics and especially the economy. What companies are doing well? What sectors are struggling? Follow the career section for news on employment and new developments in hiring practices. Always read the technology

section, which highlights new advancements and how they are changing business. I personally have a subscription so I can have access to every article, but the free online version gives just enough context that if you read it every day, within ninety days you will be better informed than most Americans. I am also an avid reader of the *Economist* and the *Financial Times*, both of which give a non-US-centric global perspective on world events.

2. TECHCRUNCH.COM — Marc Andreessen, an early pioneer in the technology revolution as the cofounder of Netscape and currently a major venture capitalist investor in Silicon Valley, famously said, "Software is eating the world."[13] When new minimum wage laws were enacted in Seattle and Los Angeles that would impact fast-food companies, what happened? McDonald's and others came out with computers that would take orders in their restaurants so they could hire fewer workers and save money. TechCrunch.com is the hub of all technology news online. From the newest tech start-ups making waves to a tech giant that is struggling, TechCrunch follows the entrepreneurs, businesses, and the impact they are having on the economy. If you want to be aware of potential changes that could radically alter your industry, company, and job, follow TechCrunch. You will be in the know about things when they are in the idea stage. You will be able to test out applications and visit websites while they are in beta (pre-launch) and it will allow you to formulate game plans on how to leverage these technologies for your business or start making plans to make a career pivot if you see it will automate your job within a few years. Be the first to move, not the last to know.

3. PODCASTS (THE RHINO SHOW, STANFORD ENTREPRENEURIAL THOUGHT LEADERS, MICHAEL HYATT, HARVARD BUSINESS REVIEW) – These free podcasts can be downloaded on your iPhone or Android device. I routinely listen to these and many more during my commute to work each day. Time is our most valuable resource, and I hate wasting even a minute. This allows me to redeem an hour of drive time each day for educational and personal development. Ryan Williams is the author of *The Influencer Economy* and host of The Rhino Show. He interviews key thought leaders in all industries. Their stories of making career pivots, starting companies, and impacting the world will inspire you on your journey while giving you great ideas. The Stanford Entrepreneurial Thought Leaders Podcast interviews industry icons and new tech start-up entrepreneurs gaining insight on new technologies and businesses that are changing the world.

Okay, I know, you're thinking: "Bob, you're telling me to listen to technology podcasts and entrepreneurial talks. This isn't me. Is this really necessary?" YES! I cannot emphasize how important this is. Secretarial and legal analyst jobs are being outsourced to India. Graphic artists, writers, and marketers are now freelancing from all over the world using Freelancer.com. I want you to know what is happening around the world and how technology will impact your career. Let your friends continue to keep their heads in the sand while you prepare. You will have success when they don't. You will bring new technologies to your

It is always better to craft your future than to wait for whatever happens.

companies and show the leadership how they can be leveraged to improve the bottom line and grow the business, thus earning promotions. Maybe the time will come that you see a technology "is" an existential threat to your job, company, or entire industry. You can read the writing on the wall and you will be able to start making your pivot into a new career field while everyone else talks about *Monday Night Football* and binges on the latest installment of Netflix or cable miniseries. Now more than ever, success is in your hands. It is up to you to work hard, be knowledgeable, and be prepared. It is always better to craft your future than to wait for whatever happens and just react. Don't be that guy!

THE POWER OF RESTORATIVE WORK

"You're not going to do good work if you're not choosing something because it inspires you."
MAGGIE GYLLENHAAL, *actress*

I could make the drive in my sleep, and many times upon arriving home, I worried that parts of the trip had been navigated in just that state. I enjoyed the winding backcountry roads from my apartment off the campus of the University of Tennessee to the local Pepsi bottling plant in Knoxville, even though my rusted Volkswagen van didn't hug the corners like the sports car I dreamed of driving one day.

I was fortunate to have a car that started with a tank of gas. I was fortunate to have a job. If everything lined up perectly I would hit my forty hours early by Thursday and get time and a half for the rest of the week. Yes, I would be tired, but when you are poor and trying to pay for college and support a wife and newborn son, time and a half is like winning the lottery.

I loved this, my first real job, but it was tough work. I would arrive at the factory late in the afternoon with the rest of the loaders. Production runs would continue through the night, but most of the employees were going home just as our shifts were beginning. A long line of semitrailers was stationed by the docks, and we would load them through the night with all the product scheduled for deliveries the next day. Grabbing a forklift, each of us would start pulling pallets of Pepsi and building special-order pallets for stores like Kroger and Food City. As a seasonal temp worker I was glad to get the job. I had never worked in a factory and never been trained to drive a forklift. Upon leaving the agency's office for my first day on the job, the manager said, "Bob, remember you can't drive any equipment. No driving of the forklifts if they ask you to do that. Do you understand?"

"Sure thing," I said, nodding my head. I was broke trying to make it through college; and despite piecing together athletic and ROTC scholarships I was still way behind each month as I tried to take care of my wife and young son. I didn't care what they asked me to do at the Pepsi plant. I needed and was prepared to say "Yes, sir" to just about anything they asked. I had been told I was hired for some office work, so I didn't think anything of this lady's comments until I arrived at the plant and my manager asked, "Have you driven a forklift before?"

I then realized they needed me for only one thing, to load semitrailers at night for delivery the next day. They explained they had lost an operator and needed me to step in . . . today. "Here is the forklift—go drive it around the back parking lot and when you are ready come back in and let's get started." Beggars can't be choosers, and I learned that in this new economy you have to be a lifelong learner, always acquiring new skills, even self-taught forklift lessons in the Pepsi plant parking lot.

Driving in the parking lot was easy. Navigating the aisles inside with other lifts and getting pallets down from the highest racks was downright dangerous. Like playing the game Operation where steady hands are needed to slowly get a bone from the playing board without hitting the edges and getting buzzed, operating a forklift is similar. I learned that without a slow, steady hand, any jerky movements would send a pallet of two liters crashing down on the cab of

Rarely are you presented with an opportunity you are 100 percent trained and prepared for.

my lift, littering the factory floor with gushing soda and an hour's worth of cleanup. This first job may not have ignited my passions, but it helped me provide for my family early in my marriage, and I learned a lot from it.

Rarely are you presented with an opportunity you are 100 percent trained and prepared for. Most often a new opportunity will require a lot of on-the-job learning, and you have to be willing to work harder than the rest and pick up new skills fast.

OLD CAREER

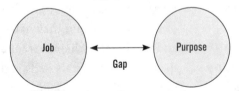

On the scale of Maslow's Hierarchy of Needs my job at Pepsi helped me fulfill the entry level of providing for the physical needs of life. And throughout my career I have been blessed to be able to pivot multiple times into new and vastly different lines of work that have allowed me to satisfy not only those basic, physiological needs but needs higher on the scale of self-actualization. These were jobs that allowed me to follow my passions and use the unique, God-given skills and talents I believe I have been blessed with. Better yet, I have been able to transition to jobs where I have a deep sense that my work is impacting others and the world, helping those in need, and inspiring people to live out their values and become the best versions of themselves through the work they do. Certainly I went through periods in my career where I felt misaligned and was not happy with my work. But I can now see how those seasons of struggle helped shape me, leading to new opportunities that would not have otherwise been possible.

NEW CAREER

Alignment of Career + Purpose

Unfortunately, many people have not been able to transition to that spot. They feel disconnected, frustrated with work, unhappy, and unfulfilled. A recent Deloitte job survey reports that 80 percent of respondents said they hated their jobs and would leave their current employer if they could.[1] Sadly, this statistic rings true to me, as many of my friends are vocal about their displeasure in their work and openly talk about the dreams of a better future, the career they aspire to but are unsure how to obtain. In a day and age where too many are unemployed or underemployed, is it okay for us to aspire to more? Is it acceptable to want a job and career that doesn't just provide for our basic needs but leverages our talents and skills, unlocks the passions inside of us, gives us purpose each and every morning, and provides an insatiable drive to do more and

> **In a day and age when too many people are unemployed or underemployed, is it okay for us to aspire to more?**

make the world a better place? The answer is yes, and it is one of the best aspects of the new economy. The world needs more people living out their passions, engaged in their work and feeling like they are making a difference in the world. Imagine if over the next decade we were able to flip the results of that Deloitte survey where 80 percent of employees loved their work and were happy and engaged. How much better and different would the world be? But before we all rush out to pivot to new things, it is best to start with a plan. We need to understand what work is, our role in work, and where our unique talents are so that we can run in the right direction.

WORK: A FAITH-FILLED WORLDVIEW

Work is such a central theme in the Christian life that we meet it at nearly every turn. The faith-versus-works tension is familiar to us: we are taught that God loves us unconditionally and that we owe God a life of excellent service. Indeed, we were made to be colaborers with God in tending the creation, and understanding how God views our work and the stewardship of resources entrusted to us is a daily concern. Most of us who care about living life as God intended have spent time praying about what specific work God wants us to do and how He wants us to do it.

However, work is often misunderstood. Some glorify work, putting it above everything else in their pursuit of riches, glory, and fame. Some tolerate work, just going through the motions because work is a means to an end. For them the saying "I work so I can live" would sum up their existence. Some people are lazy and do the least amount of work they can and would be considered average employees at best, while some refuse to work and live off society. Others are workaholics who may succeed in their careers but neglect everything else. We have a wide variety of thoughts and opinions about work, and many of them can be traced back to our upbringing. For instance, I remember a grade-school teacher instructing me that to spell "business" correctly one just needed to remember that "s-i-n" was in the middle of it. My faith journey began with this and many similarly distorted views about work from well-intentioned educators putting their spin on Scripture. With all these ideas about work, what does Scripture say about work, and how should we view the toil of our hands?

Understanding how God sees work in relation to Christian vocation is especially important today because young people who want meaningful work are facing a very rough road in a new economy. To deal with the questions of meaning and purpose that are posed by these economic realities, the world is searching for answers that can be found in the Bible. The eminent sociologist Peter Berger reports that multiple studies show that countries that were founded on Judeo-Christian values and follow the Protestant work ethic prosper economically, while other countries with different value systems lag far behind.[2]

Work was not designed to be something we loathe and can't wait to finish.

The reality is that work was not designed to be something we loathe and can't wait to finish. Work is positive, a way to create and add value to the world. It is a redemptive force in society. Economies thrive, advancements are made, people are provided for, and a virtuous cycle of improvement is a rising tide that lifts all ships in the harbor. Work is not a punishment, but an activity where we not only can provide for our needs but also gain self-worth by the activity from our hands. Most importantly, when we are in alignment with how we were created, we have the ability to restore the world around us through our efforts. I believe it is no accident that thirty-four of Christ's fifty parables in the Bible are set in the marketplace. In the book of Acts alone, thirty-seven of forty miracles are performed in the marketplace. Jesus found His greatest opportunity to help in the marketplace, and that need and that opportunity is still very much with us today.

You might be surprised by how much the Bible has to say about work, starting at the very beginning where we see God as the first worker. The Bible begins, "In the beginning *God created* the heavens and the earth" (Genesis 1:1, emphasis added), and it goes on to say, "By the seventh day God had finished *the work* he had been doing; so on the seventh day *he rested from all his work.* Then God blessed the seventh day and made it holy, because on it he rested from all the *work of creating* that he had done" (2:2–3, emphasis added).

Furthermore, God was the first employer: "God said, 'Let us make man in our image, in our likeness, so that they may rule over the fish in the sea and the birds in the sky, over the livestock and all the wild animals, and over all the creatures that move along the ground" (Genesis 1:26).

In the biblical narrative, human beings report to God as stewards: "God blessed them and said to them, '*Be fruitful and increase in number; fill the earth and subdue it. Rule over* the fish in the sea and the birds in the sky and over every living creature that moves on the ground" (1:28, emphasis added). Later it is explained, "The Lord God took the man and put him in the Garden of Eden *to work it and take care of it*" (2:15, emphasis added).

From the very start, our relationship with God was defined by the work God gave us. We are stewards or caretakers by birth to care for the things God has entrusted to us. We are to use our life, gifts, and talents to serve God and build His kingdom. There is no hierarchy of work. We are all called to be faithful in the execution of the duties we have been given, whether great or small.

In the Parable of the Talents, Christ reminds us that our stewardship will be evaluated by God. "His master replied, 'Well done, good and faithful servant! You have been faithful with a few things; I will put you in charge of many things. Come and share your master's happiness!' . . . 'And throw that worthless servant outside, into the darkness, where there will be weeping and gnashing of teeth'" (Matthew 25:23, 30).

Our work becomes worship as we glorify and honor God when we do our best. We should use the talents God has given us to expand God's kingdom by following His principles to help others and serve the poor. The apostle Paul teaches, "So whether you eat or drink or whatever you do, do it all for the glory of God" (1 Corinthians 10:31).

Whether we labor in traditional church work or the marketplace, every bit of work we do is to be ministry that reflects our service to God. I am convinced that we need committed people with the understanding of the value of work and intense work ethics in all walks of life, in every industry and career that seek to be a redemptive force in the world by using their gifts and labors of their hands to build, create, and serve society.

We should be encouraging, teaching, and empowering the next generation on their journey as stewards whose work can shine and be redemptive in a world that needs it. In truth, as we look to make a difference in the lives and world around us, this does not need to be relegated to nonprofit and charity work we might do on the side. Although that is important, the majority of our lives will be spent at work. If we are passionately living out our calling, always seeking to make the world a better place, we have a far greater opportunity to be a redemptive force for good.

Poverty or prosperity?

Not only do we need to have a proper understanding of work, and its role in our life and how it can positively impact society, but we also need to understand the results of our work. There are

God-given laws of nature that work flawlessly. Gravity treats everyone the same regardless of race, ethnicity, and religion. So, too, a law of nature is that hard work, faithfulness, honesty, and serving others will produce good results. It is just like a farmer who plants a field and tends to it. It will yield a harvest. We have entered a time where the result of those harvests is becoming highly scrutinized in the media. We hear about income inequality, the top 1 percent, and income redistribution to create economic systems that are fair. These are difficult macro-economic issues that politicians and media personalities debate. On Main Street we have similar debates on street corners and in places of worship, with people discussing two polar opposite mindsets. These can best be called the "poverty mindset" and the "prosperity mindset." As the following chart shows, these false (but widespread) ideologies are distortions of a proper view of work as stewardship. It is important that we avoid these incorrect views of work and fruits of our labor.

	POVERTY MINDSET	STEWARDSHIP	PROSPERITY MINDSET
Possessions are	evil	a responsibility	a right
I work to	meet only basic needs	serve Christ	become rich
Godly people are	poor	faithful	wealthy
Ungodly people are	wealthy	unfaithful	poor
I give	because I must	because I love God	to get
My spending is	without gratitude	prayerful and responsible	carefree and consumptive

This chart is adapted from the Crown Financial Ministries seminar, "The Bible on Money."

Even though these two incorrect mindsets are on opposite ends of the spectrum, they share the same fundamental flaw: they make what we own the most important variable—rather than whom we work for and why we work. By focusing on how much or how little we own, each of these distorted views puts the focus on us, not God. In a proper theology of work as stewardship, the focus is on God: our work is unto the Lord and we are to give our very best, leveraging the talents and skills He has given us. Results are important and they should be properly used to make the world a better place. Although it happens all the time, we should not judge each other by our titles and rank, wealth or lack thereof, or low or high position in society or at work. Only God can judge, and He is most concerned about our heart and attitudes.

Does all this mean that we will always be happy and fulfilled at work with no bad days, stress, or conflict? I wish that were the case. Those in perpetual search for an environment of rainbows and unicorns will be disappointed. Whatever our work is, we will encounter seasons of stress and difficulty. But these can be occasions for growth and refinement to prepare us for the challenges ahead. Think of the shepherd boy David in the Old Testament who was anointed as king and heralded for his feat of valor in killing Goliath. God was preparing him for leadership, and his fame and exploits angered the jealous King Saul, who tried to kill him and hunted him throughout Israel as an animal. David had to learn to wait even through the most difficult of times, as God prepared him and his men for the right time when he would be king.

For those who are praying for a new opportunity, it is important to remember that God's delays are not God's denials.

Think of Joseph, who was sold into slavery and for years toiled as a slave and was thrown into prison, yet held on to his character and integrity. Eventually he became one of Pharaoh's most trusted advisors, a man of wealth and prominence in Egypt, whose wisdom and foresight helped save an entire empire from famine. Among those saved were his family and refugees from the land of Israel.

Hundreds of years later, Moses lived as an outcast for years in the desert, herding sheep before being raised up at the right time to be the man to lead the Jews out of bondage in Egypt and back to the Promised Land. Jesus Himself had to wait years before He was able to start His ministry and let the world see the power of His hands and voice.

PIVOT EARLY IN A CAREER

A word about patience. In our world of instant gratification we too often want a "microwave career" with quick success, living our dream job without going through the years of challenges and development all successful careers require. Patience is a virtue and one of the keys to any type of career success. For those who are praying for a new opportunity, a new job, or career advancement, it is important to remember that God's delays are not God's denials. If the examples we just saw, including Jesus Himself, are any indication, it would be pretty arrogant for us to think that we would not have to go through a similar refinement and development period ourselves, correct?

I have been approached by people very early in their career who say, "I'm just not happy in my job. I am going to quit and do something different." This is great if they have a fantastic opportunity in front of them, but the mentality can also lead to job-hopping early in a career, searching for the perfect place where people are happy and fulfilled. Don't get me wrong—we all want to be happy and fulfilled. Those things are important, but it is unrealistic to think life is just easy street all the time. Work will be hard. There will be times of difficulty with the boss and with coworkers. There may even be entire seasons of life like this. Running from it will not help, and it can actually hurt you as you never develop the skills you need to acquire to be successful in the next stage of life.

I have watched people in my life who have continually run from difficulty, always taking the easy path and bailing when things get even remotely tough. Eventually they will find themselves in a midcareer cul-de-sac where it will be difficult for them to advance because they don't have any of the requisite skills and talents needed to be successful in the new economy. In the pursuit of comfort and lifestyle at the time, they turned down difficult jobs and assignments that may have required them to move, work long hours, or be a part of a company that was very demanding. By the time they wake up in the middle of their career, they will realize they enjoyed great lifestyles in their twenties but didn't accomplish much. They didn't get advanced education, didn't take the tough job, and weren't focused on gaining new skills, and in doing so have put themselves in a position where the challenges moving forward are exponentially more difficult.

The importance of "soft skills"

Soft skills include emotional intelligence, interpersonal skills, relationship building and management, conflict resolution, communication, and team building, and are not taught at most schools. They are learned primarily on the job. It has been said that a greater predictor of a person's success in this new economy is not their IQ but their EQ (emotional intelligence), and the higher you go in an organization with more responsibility the more important these skills become for your success. Soft skills are refined early in careers through trials and difficulties, and the person who continually runs from job to job because they are unwilling to face difficult challenges never develops these skills and thus hurts future career progression. These skills cannot be learned by reading a book or attending a seminar. Just as a Navy SEAL could never be fully trained in a classroom environment, to develop the critical soft skills you will need in your life requires real-world experience. So view those trials and difficult times not as something to run from but world-class training that is preparing you for bigger and more important leadership roles in your career.

The joke among many hiring agencies is that millennials want to be a part of the C-Level (CEO, COO, CIO, CFO) committee on day one, giving input on decisions, yet they have no life experience to draw upon and limited knowledge and value to give to those discussions. The best way to get asked to be a part of those discussions is to prove yourself through hard work and results. It is difficult to ignore results. If you are achieving success in your area of endeavor, you will earn your seat at the table soon enough. Earning your seat is always better than having it given to you.

Don't just jump!

I have worked with midcareer professionals who didn't have much of a life plan, and during a prolonged season of life where they were unfulfilled found themselves rushing out the door to do something different, with no idea what they were searching for. They just hoped to jump on a new opportunity that came their way. Impetuous action is never preferable to intentional design. I immediately advised them to stop and reflect on their situation to gain clarity and then to formulate a plan. The use of assessments and planning tools is a great way to gain personal insight on what steps we should take next. It is never too late to make a pivot but it is important to do it for the right reasons, with clear understanding of what we want and our goals. From there, crafting

> **We should never run from something. We should always run to something.**

a well-thought-out, detailed action plan will increase our chances of success. If you find yourself miserable with a job and you are thinking of quitting, the best advice I can give you is to be patient. Never make a decision out of anger, frustration, or when you are tired. Take a break and seek counsel from multiple people as you prepare your pivot. Sometimes people pivot not knowing what they want and end up in a similar situation, or worse. Many times the situation they are running from actually is an issue in their own life that needs to be dealt with. We should never run from something. We should always run to something. There is a very big difference.

PIVOT TO STAY

It is possible that our greatest opportunity is right where we are. We all have heard the quote that the grass is not always greener on the other side. This can be especially true in our careers when we are facing disappointment, stress, or chaos, and we have a longing to just walk out the door to start something new and by default better. When people are thinking of making a career pivot and I get the feeling it is more about them running from a perceived negative environment, I always ask if maybe a change of perspective is what they need. I know I have benefited from people helping me see different perspectives related to job situations in my career. When we are under a lot of stress or in a negative work environment and we feel powerless to change it, it is easy to see the exit door as an easy way to start over. During those times I am reminded of Paul and the extreme situations he found himself in all the while proclaiming, "For I have learned to be content whatever the circumstances" (Philippians 4:11). He is an amazing example of a man on a mission who was in a constant state of peril and discomfort, yet kept his frame of mind on being content, staying focused on the positive, and focusing on his mission. It is a great example for us to follow in our careers.

Have you ever had a big decision you struggled with, yet upon reviewing your decision after it was made it seems so obvious what the right answer was? We gain extreme clarity once the pressure and stress of making a decision is removed and we are just left with objective facts to consider. Too often we make life-altering decisions in moments of great stress. It is easy to make the wrong decision based on our emotional state and lack of total situational awareness where we take into account all the subtle decision points.

We need to remember negative situations can be temporary.

It is important when we find ourselves in moments like this to find ways to control emotions and stress to make objective decisions based on facts. During times like these I also seek counsel from advisors, coaches, or mentors in my life who have the ability to see the situation with more clarity. If we are seeking a change in our careers because of a negative situation, we need to remember negative situations can be temporary. Do we have a problem with a coworker? How can we deal with that? Before we walk out the door, have we tried to improve or remove the negative situation? It is possible during times of prolonged stress to see all the problems instead of the opportunities. Have we made a list of all the positives of our current job? It's easy to forget those and start focusing only on the negative. If you feel that you need a pivot in your mental outlook so that you can achieve your greatest potential in your current role, these are the steps I recommend.

1. FOCUS ON THE POSITIVE, NOT THE NEGATIVE—It will be easy for you to remember the frustrating points of your current job. Don't focus on those. Create a list of all the benefits of your job, your boss, the people you work with, the city you live in, etc. Focusing on those and understanding that if you leave you will be walking away from those will help you weigh the consequences of seeking a new opportunity elsewhere.

2. GET PLUGGED IN—In times of stress it is easy to cope by trying to disengage from friends and coworkers. Move in the opposite direction, spending more time with this group and seeking counsel from a mentor or coach who can help guide you through the challenge you are facing. Double down on your engagement within your organization. Being invested and committed to the organization and your team will help you navigate challenging times.

3. SET GOALS—Don't just tread water and wait for things to improve. Having goals keeps us engaged and allows us to take proactive steps to improve the situation. Action changes everything! Having organizational goals is important but you also need personal goals. How are you progressing professionally? Understand how you are making progress on your personal goals. Many times people who are unhappy in their work don't see the connection between their efforts and their personal goals. Seeing that connection is very important!

4. MAKE A DIFFERENCE—Be a part of a big project or join a team undertaking one. Get focused on the positive energy of creativity and a mission bigger than yourself. You will be consumed with the positive energy that will help offset any negativity in your work setting.

What makes a great work environment?

A great work environment is hard to find. Since we spend a majority of our lives at work, our happiness is very much connected to that culture. The following list includes things I have found in great work environments. If you have these assets as a part of your culture, don't take them for granted. These are not common. If you are seeking a new opportunity, understand the culture of your current company and the new one. I have seen people make career changes, lured away by a higher salary, only to find themselves in a negative company culture and quickly regret it. Culture is everything. Each of us has a role in growing and protecting our company culture.

Mission driven, passionately engaged—Are you passionate about what you are doing? Are you passionate about the company and what you are doing in the world? Are you making a POSITIVE difference in the world? I know people who have great jobs that produce incredible personal incomes, but their answers to the above three questions are no, and over time the emotional and spiritual toll is searing on their soul. Our work should be more than collecting a paycheck. One of the most important things to ask is if your values are in alignment with the company's values. People who work in companies where they are not aligned with leadership and company core values experience dissonance and friction, making it impossible to be fully engaged and loving your work.

Team focused—Do you love and respect the people you work with? Our coworkers become close friends and influences in our lives. If we are lucky, we get close and they become an extension of our families. We do life together. Are your coworkers people you enjoy spending time with? Do you trust them? One thing I loved about the military is the esprit de corps I enjoyed with the units I served with. I want to create that with the teams I serve with in the private sector. Having a great team environment is

> **Drama is sideways energy that prevents the organization from being successful.**

critical to our success and happiness.

Personal growth—Do you have opportunity for advancement and personal growth? Are you getting new challenges? Are you getting educational and other learning opportunities? Are you being professionally developed? Seek environments of mentorship where management cares for and is actively looking to help the staff improve and grow. These types of companies are not only great for you but that culture is the type of culture that helps companies be successful in this new economy.

No room for drama—Many times I have heard it said that "peace comes before prosperity." Drama is sideways energy that prevents the organization from being successful while searing the souls and draining the life out of everyone on the team. Some people love drama and seem to create it as a personal hobby. Do everything possible to seek work environments without drama. When there are those in your midst who cause a disproportionate amount of drama, deal with it quickly. If they cannot adjust to the team environment, it is important to help them move along. If you are in a leadership position, protect your team and company culture by removing these people quickly. If you are not in a position of authority to address these types of situations directly, have the courage to voice your concern to leadership so it can be addressed.

In conclusion, when you are looking to make a career change, make sure you are leaving for the right reasons. If you feel that part of the motivation to leave and seek something new is because of a negative situation, take a moment of pause to see if a change in your mental outlook could make a difference. Ask yourself if you have done everything to resolve the situation by making it better. The culture and work environment at your company is critical for your success and happiness. You have a hand in creating and protecting it. Understand if your company has a good environment or not and be careful when analyzing a new opportunity. Don't just consider pay rates, job titles, and other commonly analyzed data points.

PIVOT LATE IN A CAREER

I have worked with many people who are in the later stages of a career as they wind down toward retirement and realize their life plan needs a substantial pivot, because they will not be able to retire when they thought. Many people had their retirement plans completely altered after the Great Recession of 2009. Some have had to find "encore careers" to help provide additional income in retirement. Most people do not like change, but change in this season of life, especially to major life plans, can be particularly stressful and unsettling. If this is you, understand that you are not alone. From young to old, we are all in this together and we all have to adjust to this new global economy.

We have three choices. First, we can ignore it and plow forward with our plans, hoping things will be okay. I think this is the most dangerous option. Second, we can react and pivot our plans but from a position of fear or anger. This is not a healthy option either, as no one likes to live in fear and a victim mentality will prevent us from seeing, and seizing, opportunity. Our third and best option is to accept the changes that have transformed and continue to transform the economy and our place in it. We need to be intentional about learning about and understanding what's going on, then seek out the new opportunities we are being given that previous generations did not have. We can then approach these changes in life from a position of control, making pivots with excitement and anticipation for a better tomorrow.

If this is the path you wish to follow, this book has been written for you. In the coming chapters we will get granular, with action steps for your pivot, regardless of your season in life.

> ➤ **PIVOT POINTS Know Yourself and Discover Your Purpose**

Lewis Carroll, the author of *Alice in Wonderland*, once said, "If you don't know where you are going any road will get you there." Today we don't have time to waste wandering down endless paths in search of our calling, passion, and purpose in life. The routes of the past that allowed for soulful introspection while you pursued your college degree have become painfully expensive, so extending stays or getting degrees without much value is not a wise thing to do.

The routes of the past that allowed for soulful introspection while you pursued your college degree have become painfully expensive.

Furthermore, in the past, taking wrong turns early in our careers or engaging in trivial pursuits usually did not end badly. You could reenter the workforce, finding a job in a growing industry, with relative ease. Today an extended break or poor career choice can be disastrous.

Starting with a plan is the most important thing we can do. To start with a solid plan we need to understand ourselves and our God-given design. I highly recommend taking a Career Direct Personal Assessment (CareerDirect-ge.org). It is hands down the best assessment I have found to help people understand their calling in life.

For a small investment and a few hours of your time with a personal coach you will receive a thirty-three-page personal report that highlights your personality, interest, skills, abilities, and values. A personal coach will help provide next steps and resources to help you on your journey as you start to create a career and life plan. This assessment is probably the most important tool you have as you start to prepare to make a pivot in your career. We want to choose wisely and make sure that the next move, job, or career is something that is in alignment with our skills, abilities, and values. If we can tap into our passions and understand our unique, God-given design and purpose in life, we will be tapping into a well of energy and talent that will allow us to achieve our maximum potential. I believe that each person has been given a special calling in life and when we discover what that is we unleash our full potential. Career Direct will help you get alignment, find your calling, and ensure that your next pivot is successful (CareerDirect-ge.org.).

THE FOUR CAREER
QUADRANTS

"You have brains in your head. You have feet in your shoes. You
can steer yourself any direction you choose."
Dr. Seuss

As the father of six children I get a firsthand look at all sorts of
humorous childhood drama. One day a few years ago when
I came home from work, I entered the house hearing my preteen
daughter, Trista, trying to get our three-year-old to stop crying.
Finally, in frustration, Tris started to walk away from Amaris and
said loudly, "You have issues!" In the next room, the little ears of
my five-year-old, London, heard something different and she came
running in, exclaiming, "Amaris got new shoes? That's not fair! I
want new shoes too!" I then looked over to the corner of the room
where my then three-month-old daughter, Charlize, was peacefully
swinging back and forth in her baby swing, taking all of this in, and
I knew then that the estrogen factor in this house would always win.

Watching this unfold before me, seeing the drama that started
over nothing, was comical, and it reminded me of the drama that

many adults get wrapped up in on a daily basis . . . needless drama surrounding issues that don't really exist. In our home after this little incident, we coined the term "new shoes" to remind us that most of our issues are just "new shoes," something that does not exist.

Do you have issues—or new shoes? Chances are that the issues you think you have in life and in your career when analyzed from a different point of view are just "new shoes."

Having worked with many people from young college students to midcareer professionals to retirees, this phenomenon transcends all demographic boundaries. I know that about now you might be thinking you have issues. "Bob, you don't understand. My job this . . . my career that . . . my personal life . . . I can't because of . . . I wish I could . . . I am frustrated . . . It just won't work." Stop! I promise you, most if not all of the things you are experiencing are "new shoes."

> **It *is* possible that your narrative is holding you back.**

Yes, we all have real issues in our lives that are limiting factors. However, when we view these from a different perspective with the hope of a better tomorrow, the confidence that we can change our lives and directions, and the tenacity to make minor pivots until we reach our goals, any issues we have become new shoes.

I was recently interviewed on a TV show in Los Angeles about my first book, *The Leap: Launching Your Full-Time Career in Our Part-Time Economy,* and at the end of the interview I told people to email me if they would like to discuss career issues they faced. My inbox was flooded with all sorts of personal issues that were holding people back. The reality was that these had become anchors that prevented them from moving forward. They had been telling themselves for so long that they could not change because of this issue or that issue that they began to believe it. I slowly worked through the emails, trying to provide hope and encouragement to those who reached out to talk. I wanted to help change their mindset about the current circumstances they found themselves in by trying to get them to step outside the story and narrative they had crafted about their circumstances.

When we view the world differently and create a new narrative about the issues we face, that is when we can start to see new opportunities for success that we did not see in the past. I want to do that with you right now if you are thinking of putting down this book. It *is* possible that your narrative is holding you back. I promise you that by changing your story and looking at the situation from a different angle, there is a way to make your issue just become "new shoes."

REINVENT—REVECTOR—REPURPOSE—RENEW

There are four zones where we will find ourselves in life where we need to pivot. We will always be in one of the four zones of Reinvention, Revectoring, Repurposing, or Renewal.

THE 4 CAREER QUADRANTS

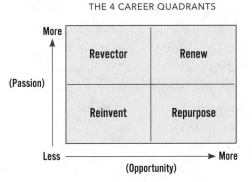

REINVENTING—There might be times in our careers where our passion for our job is gone or maybe it was never there to begin with. We also realize the opportunity for advancement and further success is limited. Sometimes this can be because the industry is changing. Employees at Kodak no doubt saw the writing on the

> **What we can or can't do is always a function of what we tell ourselves on a consistent basis.**

wall that with the invention of digital cameras there would no longer be a bright future in selling 35mm film. Maybe we realize our opportunity to advance to the next level is low because we don't have the requisite skills and education. Whether we need to reinvent ourselves because our company is in a dying market sector, or we need more education to advance, or we just want to totally change our lives and do something we have always been passionate about, a reinvention pivot is the biggest and most audacious of the pivots. It is a total life makeover. It can be difficult but it is always worth it. If you are in this zone and scared to think about it, *just remember, there are no shortcuts to any worthwhile destination*!

Example: Dreama Travis

Total reinvention of yourself and your career can be a scary process for anyone at any stage of life. For those who are late in their career this can be especially true. As I speak with people facing this challenge I often hear, "It's just too late for me. If I had to do it all over again I would do this . . . or that." What we can or can't do is always a function of what we tell ourselves on a consistent basis. Regardless of when you need to reinvent yourself in life, I hope you remember this story of Dreama.

Dreama Travis had been in the workforce since the age of eighteen, working for the past forty-one years. Since graduating from high school she had advanced up the corporate ranks in Charleston, West Virginia, and worked her way up as an executive assistant in multiple divisions of Columbia Gas. At the age of fifty-nine she continued to serve in Reston, Virginia, outside Washington, D.C. In 2002 she walked into her office and was told she was part of the massive layoff underway. Within a few weeks she would be without a job.

Losing your job is difficult for anyone, but losing it at the age of fifty-nine, as a single woman without a college education, is especially difficult. She knew her options were few; but being a hardworking, tough, and determined West Virginia girl she grew up knowing she could do anything. "Had she been born today she would be a CEO like Marissa Mayer. She broke through countless glass ceilings along the way and mentored many young ladies like me," said Pam Elder, a lifelong friend and early career mentee of Dreama. "She was one of a kind and always determined."

Part of the severance package provided by Columbia Gas gave people the option to take some classes to gain a skill or certification that would allow them to do something different as they transitioned into a new career field. Dreama decided to become a massage therapist, and shortly thereafter crafted a plan to open a bed and breakfast in the heart of the Shenandoah Valley. Seeing a simple ad in a local Washington paper that read, "For Sale by Owner. 5 Acres. Old Farm House," Dreama called the owner and bought a dilapidated old farmhouse and historic mill on the banks of the Rapidan River in Graves Mill outside of Charlottesville, and thus began the reinvention of a life at the age of sixty.

It took over a year to restore the old house and property, but soon the bed and breakfast was up and running. This was no small feat for Dreama, building a new life, a new career, a new business by herself without the help of family nearby. All the while she learned new skills of the trade, and soon the Old Mill House was recognized as a National Historic Landmark, and the bed and breakfast was winning awards for the entire state of Virginia. Weddings were routine during the summer, and guests soon became repeat visitors, bringing friends and family to enjoy the scenic views of the Shenandoah

National Forest and the quiet peace on the banks of the Rapidan. During this time of building and reinvention, Dreama became a part of the community, serving with Culpepper United Methodist Church, going on mission trips to Africa and to New Orleans after the devastation of Katrina. She would take her massage table and give back rubs to the workers rebuilding homes and helping the local population. Even with limited resources, a property that was always in need of repair, and a small business that was doing just enough to break even, she was always looking to help others around her.

I joked that she reminded me of Diane Keaton in the 1987 hit movie *Baby Boom* that highlights an executive quitting her job and moving to an old cottage in upstate Vermont, eventually starting a successful baby food company. She joked back that Diane Lane's 2003 hit movie, *Under a Tuscan Sun,* was how she liked to view herself. In that movie the heroine leaves a bus tour of Italy when she sees a crumbling villa in the countryside and buys it. Through all the disappointment that ensues, the single and resolute Diane Lane can always enjoy and count on the Tuscan sun. Dreama was certainly that, resolute and always enjoying the beauty of the local area and the people she got to meet in this chapter of her life.

Her reinvention, although difficult at the start, gave birth to one of the happiest times of her life. Little did she know this chapter would last a far-too-short thirteen years. After initially being diagnosed with cancer in 2003, she battled it on and off, until she finally passed away in the spring of 2015. I was with her during her final hours. She sat in a chair in her bedroom looking out over the property with the sounds of the rippling waters of the Rapidan, chirping birds, and the gentle mountain breezes filling her room. She was quiet and knew the end was near.

"Dreama, is there anything I can do for you?" I asked. She just squeezed my hand.

"It sure is a beautiful place you have here. You did a great job, Dreama. I am proud of you. It won't be long now. Are you excited to see Jesus?" As her energy was failing, she gave just the slightest squeeze of my hand and nod of her head. I spoke to her for a few more minutes, telling her how much I loved her and how I would take good care of her daughter and her five grandkids. Taking in the views of the life she had created one last time, she closed her eyes and soon was viewing the next life beyond.

Dreama's passing sparked an outpouring of community compassion and support. She had really made a difference in Graves Mill, and will always be remembered. Even though the historic cemetery in the village had been closed for years, the community allowed Dreama to be buried there, across from her property.

Dreama had a choice in 2002 when she learned that the life she had worked so hard for was crumbling all around her in Reston, Virginia. She could have been upset and angry. She could have quit and tossed in the towel. She instead reinvented herself, and with some hard work and determination had arguably the best time of her life, enjoyed every minute of it, and made a difference in the lives of many in the process. I am proud of my mother-in-law and the life she created for herself under tough conditions. She is an example for us all.

Points to Ponder:

1. Focus on the fact that a major disappointment (loss of a job after forty-one years in the workforce) that most people would find devastating inspired Dreama to find the silver lining and make the best out of it. She took action and reinvented herself, creating a better life that brought her new friends, joy, and fulfillment.

2. Consider the fact that gaining new skills was an important part of her reinvention.

3. Remember her courage. It has been said that courage is not the absence of fear, but rather taking action in spite of it. We will face scary situations in our careers and transitions. Our character and grit will be revealed in those moments.

REVECTORING—At times in our careers we will find ourselves doing what we love, fulfilling our calling and purpose in life, but through market changes our opportunities for advancement start to decrease. The Fisher brothers had a great love of making carriages and knew this was their passion, but saw the writing on the wall that horse-drawn carriages would become a thing of the past. They revectored to make "carriages" or automobile bodies instead. For us, revectoring might also mean moving to a new city where there are greater opportunities for our skill sets. Revectoring is an easier pivot to make than complete reinvention, as we leverage what we know and are good at to put ourselves in a better place where there is greater opportunity.

Example: Todd Williams

American distance running had a national resurgence in the 1990s, and those who followed it know the man who dominated the decade was Todd Williams. He was born in the blue-collar town of Monroe, outside of Detroit, Michigan, a place where auto factories framed the skyline. The hard-work ethic of the men and women who were the backbone of the American Industrial Revolution and the harsh winter conditions of the region were part of the DNA of the children in the area. Todd had that work ethic and drive in his DNA in spades.

He started running in 1984 in high school and fell in love with the sport. His hard work and tenacity led him to be one of the most heavily recruited athletes by his senior year and he accepted a scholarship to the University of Tennessee. From 1988 to 1991, Todd set the 10,000m record at the University of Tennessee, was an eight-time All-American, and helped the University of Tennessee win the NCAA National Championship in 1991. "I had a passion for the sport from early on and it became a career for me," Todd says, looking back upon his graduation and the beginnings of his professional career with Adidas.

From 1991 to 2002, Todd dominated distance running, winning twenty-one national championships in track, cross-country, and road racing. He earned spots on the 1992 Barcelona and 1996 Atlanta Olympic teams. One of his greatest victories was setting the National 15k record in Jacksonville, Florida, in 1995, a record that still stands twenty-one years later. When I asked him about the secret to his success, Todd replied, "I firmly believe that we all have some talent given to us from God. I think the secret of success is to take that talent and work hard. It's all about hard work. Through hard work you actually create some lucky breaks along the way, but the hard work comes first. I have heard people say, 'Well, he is naturally gifted,' or 'He has talent and I don't,' and I just don't believe it. I didn't have any more athletic talent than anyone else, but I developed an athletic mindset where I was not afraid of pain. Everyone can have that attribute. Don't think that just some successful people have it. Anyone can develop it."

As with all things in life, seasons come and go, and athletics is especially unforgiving as the athlete's mind is still ready to compete when the body starts to give way to Father Time and the abuse it has endured over the years. Todd saw the sunset of his career was upon him in 2002, but he was still passionate about the sport, even though his body was no longer able to compete at the highest levels he had previously attained. With over a decade as one of the best distance runners in the world, Todd took this momentum and his knowledge, experience, contacts, and passion for the sport and revectored into a different career.

"I went from being a professional runner to working with Adidas Marketing and Promotions from 2002–2009. I enjoyed this work, but due to budget cuts I had to transition once again—but this time into an entry-level sales position. I took the role as a sales rep for PUMA. Here I am making this transition at thirty-nine, having been a professional runner at the top of my sport, and people saw me working as an entry-level sales rep, which is normally a position for someone right out of college. People teased me about it. It was hard, and I had to be humble to do this.

"It turned out to be one of the most important transitions of my life. I worked hard to prove everyone wrong. Inside, I battled doubt and wondered if I was doing the right thing. We all have those battles to deal with, regardless of what profession we are in."

Todd worked with PUMA for two years and then was offered a position back at Adidas as a Running Tech Rep working with local stores. He learned the retail trade as he helped customers and heard their needs in communities all around the country. "A lot of sales reps when they are on the road go out drinking after a long day. I still had that athletic spirit in me and needed to dedicate my spare time to do something better. I picked up Brazilian Jujitsu and started training every day at different gyms around the country."

Todd added, "As I was working for my black belt in this new sport, I was seeing how safety was a big concern for the average citizen out exercising each day. This is especially true for students on college campuses. In four years I had been learning everything I could about the retail operations and needs of customers while I was honing my craft of personal defense and it just came to me. This is a perfect intersection of what I am passionate about and there is a big need for this in communities everywhere. I started asking people if I could hold self-defense workshops and tested out my theory and it was a slam-dunk. People loved it and that is when RunSafer was born in January 2013."

Todd combined his love and knowledge of running with his new passion for Brazilian Jujitsu and self-defense, and created a safety company dedicated to training and educating exercise enthusiasts on how to protect themselves. Asics now sponsors Todd to travel the country to conduct self-defense seminars in local running stores. Todd also conducts these same classes for college athletic programs around the country, helping college athletes be aware of their surroundings and know how to defend themselves if attacked. (If you would like to learn more about a RunSafer program in your area, check out RunSafer.com.)

Revectoring is the art of taking the momentum, contacts, and knowledge you have in your career and making slight alterations to leverage it for something different. Todd is a perfect example of this. Today Todd has taken a lifetime of knowledge and experience along with his passions for the sport and is giving back, helping make communities safer.

One might think that Todd settled for this next chapter of life as it could not be as exciting as winning national championships and hearing the crowds in Olympic stadiums cheer him on, but those people would be wrong. "As I get older it is so much more important to me to serve and give back. I find so much more fulfillment in doing it. Helping people is so much more important to me than all the awards I won in my career." Todd went on to say, "It can take people a long time to realize this but the truth is that helping people and making a difference in the world is so much more rewarding than any award you can achieve for yourself. I have learned that is where true happiness is."

Todd is a class act. I have known him since 1993 and he was the reason I went to the University of Tennessee to run track and cross-country from 1993–1998. He has been a coach and friend who has had a positive impact on my life. I have seen him live the principles he teaches. As I closed out the interview with him, I asked, "Todd, what advice would you give someone who might have just lost their job or has had some bad career news and is thinking about Revectoring in their career like you did?" After a brief pause to reflect, he said, "Everyone has to be the one to develop their own plan and be dedicated every day to take on that plan. No one will do it for you or want it more than you. Don't surround yourself with negative people who will pull you down. Get people who will help and inspire you. You also have two choices when something bad happens: you can say, 'Man that sucks,' and wallow in it, or you can say, 'Man that sucks . . . okay, I'm going to kick butt tomorrow.' Attitude is everything!"

Points to Ponder:

1. Focus on Todd's work ethic ("hustle") in every stage of his career. It is a common theme for success. Regardless of who you are or how much talent you think you have, hard work is the most important.

2. Consider Todd's humility to take a step backwards in the middle of his career. It was that step that helped him launch a new career.

3. Remember Todd's desire to learn everything he could about retail when he was given that opportunity. That knowledge led him to be able to launch a business in the retail space, serving customer needs that were not being addressed.

REPURPOSING—The opposite of Revectoring is Repurposing. This is when we might be in a situation where we have all sorts of opportunity with incredible prospects of future growth and income potential, but our heart is just not in the work. We know that we are out of alignment and that we were called to do something different or to have a bigger impact in the world. Repurposing is one of the easier pivots because we are generally making the pivot from a stronger financial position and on our own terms. Unlike getting fired from a job or suddenly realizing our company is going out of business and being in a reactive mode, in this stage we are in a pro-active mode, seeking out something that is in alignment with our skills, passions, and true calling in life. I have witnessed attorneys pivoting from the legal profession to become ministers, executives pivoting into nonprofit work, and entrepreneurs selling family businesses they inherited to start something that was truly their own.

Example: Daniel Headrick

Daniel Headrick had achieved the American dream, or so it seemed. The gifted young professional was just a few years out of law school at the age of thirty-one and had just been offered to be partner at a prestigious law firm in Knoxville, Tennessee. At the same time, his wife, Jenney, a doctor, was being offered the position of partner in her local medical practice. From the outside, this idyl-lic all-American success story hid the private discussions between a husband and wife who against all traditional wisdom were about to make a radical decision. Daniel was about to walk into his firm and turn down the offer and quit his career so he could go to seminary at Baylor University. Jenney would support him and do the same and move with him to Waco, Texas. "I started to feel I was called to do something different and over time I realized I had to make the move," said Daniel, remembering the moment they made the decision to repurpose their lives.

Daniel had received his undergraduate degree in Religious Studies and a master's degree in Philosophy with a Religious Studies concentration from the University of Tennessee. "My goal had been to go on and get a PhD and teach secular religion at a university," said Daniel. "I was accepted into a top five program at Duke, but I didn't want to take out $250,000 in student loans over the next seven years to fund that study. Making a purely logical decision for economic reasons, without seeking guidance or praying about it, I chose to go to law school at UT." Daniel graduated from the University of Tennessee School of Law in 2007 and spent the next six years practicing civil litigation tort defense and had achieved great success.

"I was basically an agnostic. I had been brought up in the Christian faith but was not practicing it. As my daughter was coming of age, I knew I wanted to give her an identity and community. My journey began when I met Pastor Bill Sheill in Market Square when I was thirty-one. He was an intellectual Christian and his mentorship and our discussions helped me to start asking questions and researching things. A transformation began in my life." The long road of transformation was taking place and in a few years Daniel was feeling restless at work. "Obviously not everyone who has a religious experience is then called to ministry but that is what was going on in my life. I felt I was being called. I sat down with my wife over dinner and told her, and she realized that it was real and I wasn't joking." Daniel and Jenney embarked on a three-month journey of talking and asking questions. Was this just a midlife crisis? Was he really going to turn his back on a successful law career and go back to school for four years of seminary and then into full-time ministry? As they opened up to some people about this decision, there were some who thought he was crazy! They were living the American dream. "Unlike in the previous decisions in my life, I was really praying about this one and seeking God's direction. One day I received a sign from God and I knew in my heart that I was called. But this was a big decision and I knew Jenney had to be on board as well. It had to be a joint calling. Without her I could not have done it. When she said she would support me, I knew it was final."

On the day that Daniel was officially offered the prestigious designation of partner at his law firm, he let them know that not only would he not accept but he was leaving the firm to go to seminary and to repurpose his life in a new career pursuit. The law firm was more than gracious in allowing Daniel to remain at the firm for almost a year with the understanding that he would leave for seminary. "After I made the decision, I had a lot of doubts. I began to feel unworthy of a calling like this. Who am I to be a minister? It was at this moment that Pastor Tom Ogburn told me, 'Daniel, no one is worthy when they are called. Who benefits when you think you are not worthy?' It was encouragement like that and support from my wife and others who helped me stay the course. I was at a point where anyone could have blown this up because of my self-doubt, but everyone was so affirming."

Daniel's calling was strong, and through prayer and support of those around him he repurposed his career, making a massive, life-altering change. "I had come to realize that I was wrong about what my personal story was. I had made wrong decisions based on that story and I had to be okay with being wrong and wanting a different story for my life going forward."

Daniel is finishing up his last year at Truett Theological Seminary at Baylor University. I asked him what he has learned from this process and what advice he would give to people who may be hearing a new calling in their lives. "First, I would tell people to be very cautious to see things in black-and-white terms. For example, that you are leaving one career to do another and that those previous chapters are closed forever. I have found that I have been able to practice law while I am in school and I am getting unique opportunities to serve my former firm in different ways. I didn't see that as an option early on. Second, don't view career decisions or other decisions as mistakes in your past. See them as experiences to get you to your true calling. I see my past and all the things I went through and my law career not as a mistake but as affirming.

It helped prepare me for this challenge in front of me. Finally, I did things backwards. I picked my vocation and later in life I discovered my calling. This happened after I became a true follower of Jesus. We are called to be disciples first and foremost and that impacts every other aspect of our lives. When we get this right understanding, our vocation and calling will be easy."

Points to Ponder:

1. Focus on how Daniel says that our vocation should be subordinate to discipleship. Do you have a true understanding of discipleship? Do you see your vocational calling through your role as disciple?

2. Consider Daniel and Jenney and their willingness to make big career sacrifices to follow the calling they had discerned. Are you prepared to make sacrifices if called to do so? What groups of people would you look to for support and encouragement during that time?

3. Remember that Daniel said he felt this was a "joint calling." He could not do this alone. He did not force Jenney to follow him but left it up to her to make this decision with him. If you are married, these big career decisions must be made together as a team. Don't force your will or dreams on your spouse. Let them be an equal part of the decision-making process and listen to what they may be hearing and discerning as well. Secondly, remember that Daniel said not to see things in black and white. Look for the best in your past, as it oftentimes is part of your future.

RENEWING—Ephesians 4:21–24 says, "When you heard about Christ and were taught in him in accordance with the truth that is in Jesus. You were taught, with regard to your former way of life, to put off your old self, which is being corrupted by its deceitful desires; to be made new in the attitude of your minds; and to put on the new self, created to be like God in true righteousness and holiness."

So too in our careers we should all aspire to be in the state of constant renewal. When we achieve this, we are maximizing our pas-

Today's opportunity can become tomorrow's also-ran.

sions/skills/purpose in life and are full of energy and excitement, knowing we are operating on a plan and achieving what we were meant to do in life. We are also in a zone of high opportunity and impact, so our efforts are making a difference in the world and with others around us, while at the same time providing for our needs and advancement of our careers.

Once we are in the sweet spot of our career, we must always be vigilant to daily work hard to stay there. The world is quickly changing around us, and we must always be on the lookout for changes that could impact our jobs, company, or industry. Today's opportunity can quickly become tomorrow's also-ran. Yahoo is a living example of this.[1] The world passed it by and it did not renew fast enough. Those working there once were at the cutting edge of the Internet revolution, but now their future opportunities are vastly different and more limited.

Life is all about cycles. This is why this stage is called "renewal." It is not finished. To stay here we must continually be in a state of personal development, growth, and learning; otherwise we can fall into one of the other three zones. My college coach used to tell us track athletes that it is easier to stay in shape than to get into shape. The older I get, the truer those words are. The same is also true in our careers. Getting into our sweet spot, in the zone, and in the state of renewal can be challenging. Once we are there, it is important to work hard to stay there by never resting on our laurels and thinking we have arrived.

THE ZONE OF RENEWAL

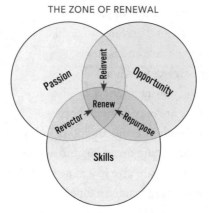

Example: Several at the top of their game

The zone of renewal is where we all aspire to be. We have reached a sweet spot in our careers where instead of looking to transition to new, more fulfilling work, we long to capture the moment because we know we are in the right spot and loving every minute of it. Our biggest concern should be how to stay at the top of our game. How do we continue to improve mentally, physically, emotionally, and spiritually so that we can be our best and optimize our performance?

Due to the complex nature of this zone, it is impossible to have one example. Therefore I will highlight a composite of individuals who I believe are showing the traits of personal renewal to stay at the top of their game in their respective fields.

In our careers, especially today with the quickly changing global markets, renewing most often means adding new skills and competencies to our tool belt to stay ahead of change. Regardless of the stage in our careers, it is important to build this into our daily routine. Take, for example, my friend Drayton Wade, who graduated with honors from Clemson and received his master's with distinction from the prestigious London School of Economics.

During a yearlong internship program in Knoxville, in his personal time he took free MOOC courses online from the University of Michigan because he wanted a better understanding of complex forms of finance.

While his peers partied, he studied.

While his peers partied, he studied. Months later the CEO of a new tech company offered him a prized role on the ground floor.

Jordan Mollenhour is a venture capitalist. In his midthirties, married with kids, he is already successful with a growing company. He holds three degrees from the University of Tennessee (BA in Business, MBA in Business, and JD in Law). He has decided to attend the prestigious University of Pennsylvania Wharton School of Business to receive another MBA. "Why?" you might ask, and so did I.

"I know that in this economy knowledge and connections are everything. This program will allow me to meet a new group of leaders, and the decisions I am making now in my business are big. If I am able to refine my thinking at Wharton and I am able to make just one or two better business decisions in my career, it could be worth millions of dollars. It is totally worth it," said Jordan.

Heather Stanfield is another example. She is the director of marketing at Crown, and I love working with her. She took an advanced marketing course at Northwestern University's Kellogg School of Business to help her stay sharp and refine her skills in her role. Another example is Grant Webster, a young millennial who started a tech company in Ohio, who recently told me he hired an executive coach to help him become a better leader and manage his team and company better. He also routinely goes to conferences around the country like SXSW to obtain new ideas and stay in touch with changes in technology that will impact his customers.

Renewal is not always about intellectual knowledge. Chris Swanson is a sheriff in Michigan and part-time motivational speaker and coach. His expertise is helping people maximize physical fitness and achieve greater results of renewal in that area of life. Jermeie Kubicek, the author of *5 Voices*, is helping people be more emotionally aware and present in their speech with friends, family, and coworkers. Andrew Huck, cofounder of GS Capital, is concerned with the spiritual well-being of members of his community, holding weekly Bible studies at lunch for local business people to talk about the issues they are facing while allowing them to create a support network for each other.

In the zone of renewal, to have success one must be observant and take intentional action. We have to be honest with ourselves and understand where we have weak spots and take action to fix them—educationally, physically, spiritually. We need to see where our industry is heading and know what will be critical for our success in the future and prepare ourselves and those around us.

CYCLE OF SELF-IMPROVEMENT

Those who are winning daily fight the status quo. Many people have their lives on "cruise control." People in this zone broke that switch a long time ago. In the Air Force we have a term called the OODA loop. Fighter pilots are taught to Observe, Orient, Decide, Act.[2] To move into a high state of personal renewal that becomes a part of your daily life, you need to incorporate a personal

OODA loop in all areas of your life. Observe all aspects of your life. Orient yourself to know how they fit together into the overall mosaic of your life. Decide what things need to be worked on and why. Where are you strong and where are you weak? The most important step, Act! Devise clear and easy-to-understand plans and take daily intentional action to make improvements.

Fighter pilots are taught to Observe, Orient, Decide, Act.

You will be amazed at the improvements you are able to make in ninety days. If you run the OODA loop for a year, you will be amazed at the results you can achieve.

Points to Ponder:

1. Focus on the multiple examples of adding skills and education regardless of age and where the person is in their career. There is always a way to improve.

2. Consider your strengths and weaknesses. Never work on just one. Continue to improve in all areas. What are the skills you need to refine for the next stage of your career or personal life?

3. Remember, this should become a lifelong process. This is not a quick fix. To achieve lasting results, run the OODA loop constantly and look for new ways to grow and improve.

"BELIEF IS THE BIGGEST PART OF SUCCESS."
—TONY DUNGY

Have you ever been in a situation in your career where you were struggling, intensely unhappy, feeling trapped? Did it seem like there was no way out? Maybe you watched others have success and you felt like you were Moses out in the desert, tending sheep in isolation with no way of ever making a difference and getting back into the game. Maybe the story of Joseph resonates with you when he was doing the right thing but was jailed and no one believed in him. Maybe you feel like you are trapped in your own proverbial jail. In a job you dislike but you don't feel like you have any other options. People tell you, "Just be happy you have a paycheck. Look at the unemployment numbers and decrease of earnings for workers over the past thirty years! You should be grateful," but deep down inside you feel guilty

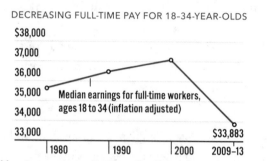

DECREASING FULL-TIME PAY FOR 18-34-YEAR-OLDS

Median earnings for full-time workers, ages 18 to 34 (inflation adjusted)

$33,883

Graph adapted from *Fortune* magazine, "A Millennial's Field Guide to Mastering Your Career" by Clarie Groden, January 1, 2016.

for yearning for more. But more than the guilt, you feel the weight of the world on your shoulders, the responsibilities and stress of your job, and people you just don't enjoy working with. If we are all honest, at some point in our careers, even if it is just for a day, most of us have experienced this to some degree. Then the phone rings or you open up your email and there is an amazing opportunity in front of you. Remember that feeling? You could almost levitate. It seems like your prayers have been answered and as you drive home you consider the possibilities, the new adventures, the opportunities, the new challenges, and it is like you are living a different life, all because of a new opportunity where you were sought after by another company who wanted you, valued you, and was desperate to have you on their team. The hope for a better future is intoxicating. The feeling of knowing you are valued, appreciated, and wanted is more than any pay raise or bonus you could earn.

For those of you who have experienced this, close your eyes for a moment and think back to that time and remember the feeling. For those of you who have not experienced it yet, imagine it. Why is the pivot important? Because there comes a time in all our careers where we will need to make a pivot because we find ourselves in one of the zones above. The longer we stay in the Reinvent, Revector, and Repurpose zones with the desperate need to move on or do something else, the more painful our experiences become, and the more joy and elation we will experience when we actually make the pivot into a new chapter of our life. Our goal is to be in the Renewal zone! For those who feel trapped and stranded in a cul-de-sac of their career, I want you to experience this renewal. This is why we need to make the pivot.

When we are alone and focusing on the past, we tend to focus on the negative and craft a narrative around perceived issues that are really just "new shoes," and soon we begin to believe those limiting factors and we allow them to hold us back. When we understand what is happening in the world around us and craft a plan with actionable items and start taking baby steps in the direction of our future, we experience the liberating joy and excitement in the power of hope for a better tomorrow.

> ➤ **PIVOT POINTS** A New Perspective

In chapter 1, our action plan consisted of developing a routine of getting plugged in by gaining new knowledge of the global economy and major trends by reading certain periodicals, listening to podcasts, and reviewing important websites. In chapter 2 our action plan was to get a deep-dive personal analysis of our skills, passions, and values with a Career Direct assessment. In this past chapter we learned which one of the four quadrants we currently find ourselves in our careers. With this information, our next action step is to get a personal one-on-one consultation with a trained advisor to help us start to put these pieces of the puzzle together and craft a career plan.

Many times I have people contact me via email asking how they can find a coach or mentor to help them in their career. The reality is that there rarely will be just one person who will be able to help us navigate our entire career. The most successful people I know leverage the skills and insight from a multitude of advisors. You will certainly have many people who will be able to help you on your journey, but right now I think the most important advisor is a Career Direct consultant who has been trained on the assessment you have taken. I highly recommend signing up to get a personalized two-hour session to go over your results. Let them know which one of the career quadrants you are in and what you think your frustrations are as well as your goals. There are over 2,200 trained consultants globally, operating in over eighty nations and in twenty-two different languages, helping people each day navigate career issues. Many people personally contact me asking for help, and I always get them started with a Career Direct assessment and consultation. I have never had a negative response. As I said earlier, sometimes we need a different perspective from someone who can see things more clearly and without the stress and emotion of our current situation. The guidance and clarity of a Career Direct consultant has helped hundreds of thousands of people pivot to the next chapter in their lives based on sound analysis. This is our next action step. You can get your consultation at www.CareerDirect-ge.org, and a detailed thirty-three-page report and action plan designed for you.

KNOWING YOUR TRANSCENDING CAREER SKILLS

"A winner is someone who recognizes their God-given talents, works their tail off to develop them into skills, and uses these skills to accomplish their goals."

LARRY BIRD

Some might think the pristine rolling hills, beautiful countryside, and year-round perfect weather of Palo Alto are prime reasons for attracting the most brilliant minds from around the world to attend Stanford University, but that is just an ancillary benefit to those who aspire to attend this world-changing institution. Nestled in the heart of Silicon Valley, Stanford has given birth to many of the tech start-ups that are rewriting how we live, interact, and view the world.

With a majority of the student body in technical fields like engineering, and in close proximity to the venture capital hub of Silicon Valley, it is no surprise that a recent article in the *Wall Street Journal* highlighted that of the top business schools in the world, Stanford ranks first in current students launching their own companies, with over 16 percent starting a company while in school.[1] With some of the best teachers in the world and access to venture capitalists looking to help aspiring young entrepreneurs launch the next Google, Microsoft, Amazon, or Uber, is it any wonder that the school in Silicon Valley is transforming the world?

However, the greatest skills and lessons being learned by many of these young people are not taught within the university system.

On a fall afternoon in 2015, students crowded into a classroom on Stanford's campus to hear from three prominent thought leaders in their field. This talk was recorded for the Stanford Technology Ventures Program Podcast. Steve Jurvetson, venture capitalist from DFJ; Astro Teller from Google X; and Christina Smokle, associate professor of bioengineering and chemical engineering at Stanford, held court, answering questions from the students and offering perspective on the future of technology. Steve Jurvetson opined on the fast-changing state of technology and how it is impacting everyone. For example, Moore's Law, a universally understood law in technology, states that on average the number of transistors that can fit on a microchip doubles every twenty-four months. The impact of this means that computing power continues to get faster and also cheaper at the same time. Phones will continue to advance to do more and more.

"Stuff you are learning now is going to be irrelevant in ten years."

Things that could not be automated a few years ago are now within our reach, like self-driving cars and clothing with embedded chips that monitor our health and provide user data instantly to our smartphones. Looking globally, Wi-Fi systems that cover every inch of the earth are closer than ever before.

Let me help you connect the dots. Industries will quickly be born, replacing industries (jobs) of the past. Emphasizing the need to be aware and understand how this would impact all the students listening, Steve Jurvetson said, "We are in an era of ever-accelerating change. . . . The life span of anything is more and more ephemeral. Your career and lifelong learning becomes all the more imperative. How can I pivot to something new from something I have already done?"[2] It was not long before Astro Teller, the man in charge of the secretive Google X department, the department engineering "moon shot" projects like the driverless cars among many other things, said, "Stuff you are learning now is going to be irrelevant in ten years. . . . Be prepared for that . . . the skill of learning things quickly . . . [is] critical for the rest of your life."[3]

We will all have to develop new sets of expertise over time. To do this we need to have a set of foundational, transcending career skills upon which we will build new careers and leverage new opportunities. These skills will never be outdated and will never give way to technological change or automation. Build and leverage these skills to set yourself apart from the crowd and position yourself for lifelong success.

1. Hustle (earlier generations called this "work ethic"!)
2. Problem Solving
3. Situational Awareness (seeing the bigger picture, connecting the dots)
4. Emotional Intelligence (often called soft skills or people skills)
5. Communication (storytelling, motivating, influencing)
6. Lifelong Learning (the process of quickly acquiring new skills)
7. Character and Integrity

Hard to teach in the classroom, these types of skills are learned through practice and from mentors giving guidance and perspective. It is a journey of growth through trial and error and life experience. Once learned, they transcend all career fields and

In the Air Force, one of our core messages was "Service Before Self," and this tied directly to work ethic.

industries, enabling the possessor to be highly marketable, desirable by any company, with the ability to pivot quickly into any industry. These skills are the same that everyone can and should be acquiring right now in our daily lives, regardless of what industry we are in or education background we come from. In this chapter we will dive deeper into each area with practical ways to develop these skill sets.

HUSTLE: ABOVE AND BEYOND FOR THE MISSION

"We are what we repeatedly do. Excellence, then, is not an act but a habit." —ARISTOTLE

This is the very first and most basic building block for success. Those people with a strong work ethic are easy to spot, and rise to the top in any organization. They quickly become the "go-to" people that leaders trust to get the most important projects done where failure is not an option. In the Air Force, one of our core values was "Service Before Self," and this tied directly to work ethic. No matter what we had going on in our personal lives, the commitment to our mission was first and foremost. When I work with people who have been in the military, we generally all have that same baseline understanding that mission is first. There is a pride to working hard and doing whatever it takes to get the job done. I have seen this in the private sector as well, and seek out team members who have that "can-do" spirit. In discussions with a number of CEOs in a forum in YPO (Young Presidents Organization), we often share ideas on how to work with young millennials who, when interviewing, appear most concerned with work/life balance and vacation time offered, and are the first to bolt out the door in the afternoon regardless of what is happening in the office. This type of attitude inadvertently tells the company that your personal life is more important than your job, and that you are not committed to the organization's success and are not willing to go above and beyond to accomplish the mission.

This is the wrong message to send. Yes, work/life balance is important, and any good leader will work hard to ensure their staff is adequately taken care of. These organizations are easy to spot during the interview process; you can learn a lot about a company by getting a sense of their culture. Work/life balance is important, but remember this—in this new, fast-changing economy, those without a strong, demonstrable work ethic are not going to be at the top of any hiring list and will be the first ones to be let go from a company. One CEO of a national executive placement firm became so frustrated at the continued talk about work/life balance at his company that he called a company-wide meeting and said, "People need to understand that on average the standard workday here is about ten hours to get the job done. Our jobs are to serve our clients and if something is going wrong, you need to be willing to work as long as it takes to serve the customer, even if that is twelve to fourteen hours a day until the crisis is over. That is what the clients are paying you for. In today's economy it is expected of all of us. Those not willing to give our customers that level of support . . . this job is not for you."

As I speak with more and more CEOs around the world, that is the level of commitment that is expected from them by their boards, and that is what they expect from key staff. Everything goes in seasons, of course, and rarely do you find an organization that calls on people to routinely work fourteen hours a day. However, you need to be able to flex to that degree, should your company need you for a crisis of short season. Doing so highlights your work ethic and, even more important, commitment to the mission.

Most CEOs I speak with decry the decay of many people's work ethic today. They say there is a sense of entitlement and many times an "I don't care" attitude among employees who are just there to collect a paycheck and get home as quickly as possible. Many times this is a function of the culture that has been created and accepted at a company. This type of culture is an early warning sign that the company is headed for trouble. If it is a strong company with a dominant market position, this hubris will allow their competitors to pass them by. If the company is weak and struggling, this type of culture all but predicts their further demise. You can't rise from the ashes when people don't care and are checking out. Many reports are now coming out that this was the culture of Yahoo.com in its final years before it was finally sold to Verizon. If you work in such an environment that has this type of culture, displaying an amazing work ethic will go a long way. Arriving early, being prepared for the day, doing a great job, not wasting time or resources, when finished with a task volunteering to help others or taking on additional tasks to help the organization or your boss, staying late to help others or to get a head start on other projects are all surefire ways to get noticed and rise to the top quickly. If people with an incredible work ethic are hard to find, it will not be difficult for you to be the unicorn, easily spotted by leadership by demonstrating your ability to work harder than everyone else. All industries and companies need these types of performers. People with this work ethic rise to the top in any career field and, as my father used to teach me, "The harder you work, the luckier you get!"

EMPLOYEES – TOP PERFORMERS

Poor Performers	Average	Top Performers
5–10%	70%	15–20%

PROBLEM SOLVING: "FIRE AND FORGET"

"A problem well defined is a problem half solved." —CHARLES KETTERING, *American inventor, holder of 186 patents, founder of Delco*

To become a top performer, it's not just about working harder; it is also about working smarter. Regardless of where you are in the corporate structure in your organization, from entry-level employee to senior executive, those you answer to have a myriad of problems to solve. In the Air Force we had a term, "Fire and Forget," which came from fighter pilots who had to train to engage multiple enemy targets at once. With certain weapon systems like radar and heat-seeking missiles, once locked on the target they were able to "fire and forget," knowing the missile would do its job and they could turn their attention to another target. In the military and in the business world, leaders are looking for people who can problem-solve and get the job done without having to be monitored every second for input and direction. This person allows them to "fire and forget" so they can move on to the next task, knowing that they don't have to think about it any longer and the mission will get accomplished. People who earn this designation and level of trust with their supervisors are worth their weight in gold and over time can command a king's ransom for their services because they are so rare. If I have an employee where I have to be in on every decision and constantly give direction, I have not freed up much of my time, and it limits my effectiveness for my organization.

On the other hand, there are many leaders who love this level of involvement. We know them as "micro-managers." They get a sense of security and validation from being a part of all the details. If you have a staff member who is incompetent or failing at the job, you might have to engage like this for a short while to help them, but it is not ideal and certainly not over the long term. Team members who have gained trust, know the job well, know how the leadership thinks, understand the culture of the organization, and what the end objectives are can start to operate as problem solvers for the organization and this allows the leader to "fire and forget" projects over to you.

Learning how to do this is as easy as following this four-point process. First, you have to *understand the problem*. A well-defined problem is the key to a successful outcome. What are you trying to fix? What isn't working? What needs improvement?

Second, you need to *know the desired outcome*. You need to take something from a current state to a different state. In a perfect world, what is that? Does your product need to perform better? Does customer service need to improve? Does a new product need to be developed to solve a customer problem?

With the start and end now clearly defined, it is just a matter of problem-solving the steps and resources needed to get there. In a perfect world you will not have any issues, but in the world in which we operate there will always be "lim-facs" or "Limiting Factors." There will be constraints on time, money, and quality. This is the third step, where your problem solving will be put to the test to understand what the organization's limiting factors are and how to work within the constraints you have been given to solve the problem and accomplish the mission.

The fourth and final point is the *feedback loop*. How engaged does your supervisor need or want to be in the project? This is not something you can determine yourself but needs to be asked. The level of company investment required and how important the project is to the overall success of the strategy of the organization will determine how often your supervisor or senior team will want feedback and progress reports. Let them determine this for you; then come to each meeting with a fully developed status report, having thought out the most likely questions they will ask, with your answer ready. If there are problems, give them your ideal solutions so they see that you have taken the initiative to think it through.

Intellectually lazy people will come to these meetings presenting problems without offering solutions, waiting for their boss or senior team to come up with the solution. This is one of the most career-damaging things you can do. Highlight your thinking and problem-solving ability by giving options. If they select your proposed solution, fantastic. If not, they get to offer insight and perspective, and the dialogue of the solutions will help you see how your leaders think, and they in turn can mentor you along the way. Critically for you and your organization, interactions like this build trust.

SEEING THE BIGGER PICTURE: CONNECTING THE DOTS

"Details create the big picture."
—SANFORD I. WEILL, *former chairman, Citigroup*

At the turn of the twentieth century, Charles Steinmetz (1865–1923), famed mathematician and technological pioneer, was world renowned for his theories of alternating power that enabled the expansion of the electrical grid and electrical power industry we know today. Engineers at General Electric were having problems with one of their massive generators in upstate New York. Not

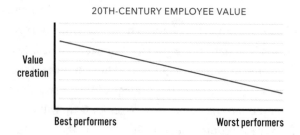

20TH-CENTURY EMPLOYEE VALUE

Value creation

Best performers   Worst performers

knowing how to fix the problem, they called in Mr. Steinmetz as a consultant to review the plans and give advice. After a lengthy time of studying the blueprints of this massive machine, Charles left the engineering room to see the generator firsthand. He carefully placed an "X" on a small section of tubing and wrote a set of instructions to cut it out and replace the wiring inside, and then departed. General Electric's engineers performed his instructions and fixed the machine. Later, General Electric was shocked upon receiving notice of his $1,000 fee, which was astronomical for that era. They asked for a detailed invoice for the work, upon which Charles Steinmetz replied with "$1 for making the X and $999 for knowing where to make the X." His invoice was paid.

This story has been told many times, including a 1999 commencement address at the Massachusetts Institute of Technology by president Charles Vest, highlighting the value of seeing how all the pieces of the puzzle fit together.[4] In the old industrial economy, the difference between the best and worst performer was marginal. For example, in a manufacturing context it has been said that the best performers on a production line might be able to outperform an average performer by three or four times. However, in the new information age knowledge workers can outperform an average programmer producing a thousand times and more value for a company. Don't take my word for it, founder and former CEO of Microsoft Bill Gates has been quoted as saying, "A great lathe operator commands several times the wage of an average lathe operator, but a great writer of software code is worth 10,000 times the price of the average software writer."[5] In the old economy, there was certainly a difference between the best and worst performers but in our new economy that difference has been magnified sometimes a thousandfold. Great opportunities, jobs, rewards, and wealth will be available to those who are the top performers in this new economy. Furthermore, to contextualize this in a different way it has been said that those who understand *how* will always work for those who understand *why*. Greg Barnes, president and founder of Halftime Talent Solutions, confirms the idea: "Put two résumés side by side that are almost identical, and the person who understands the big picture of the business, how things inter-relate and work, will be paid three times more than the person who just knows the specifics of their area."

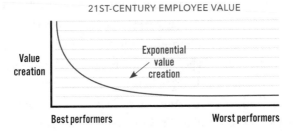

21ST-CENTURY EMPLOYEE VALUE

This is a perfect way to show why understanding the bigger picture is so important. It is imperative to be proficient at your job and to have a deep understanding of any systems or endeavor you are responsible for. However, many people are satisfied to stop there and to be domain experts in that niche. The secret is to never be satisfied and to take the time to dig deeper and to learn how other aspects and disciplines of your business are connected. How does your company serve its customers and provide value? Where are the trouble spots that senior management is working on or worried about? What is going on in your industry? Who are your biggest competitors? What are they doing right? What are they doing wrong? Where is there new opportunity that people don't see? Where is your organization excellent? Where are you falling behind? What do your customers rave about? What do they complain about? These are all questions that will help you see the bigger picture.

You can't solve problems unless you know what they are and can see the forest through the trees. Most people will be content to come to work each day keeping their head down and doing the minimum required to be successful in their particular department, then head home at the end of the day. Those who dig deeper have a leg up on all the competition.

Two things to remember here. Yes, it is a competition. There are limited resources for raises and advancements in any company, and those who demonstrate work ethic, problem solving, and the ability to see the big picture and understand how things work will have greater opportunity than those who just want to do the minimum required. Why will *you* have this opportunity? Most people are not willing to put in the work to do this because it will require working longer and harder. It will require you being willing to put in extra time when others go home and are socializing. An early mentor of mine used to say, "Bob, being successful in life is easy because so many people are willing to accept average. Anyone going above and beyond in the pursuit of excellence is competing against very few people, and success is almost guaranteed." Success over those who are willing to be average is certainly guaranteed if you are driven for excellence.

So how do you train yourself to see the bigger picture and to be able to connect the dots on the important issues inside your company and outside your industry? First, *you need to have margin built into your life to research and learn*. Learning about the rest of your company, how all the parts connect to create value to your customers, is critical. Volunteer to help other departments on projects. Take on special tasks and projects the senior leadership team is working on. Ask questions and whenever possible try to earn a seat at the table where decisions are being made. Listen and take great notes, and when you don't understand, don't be afraid to ask for clarity on things.

Learning about your *industry* is just as important, especially if you have a goal to pivot to a new job or another company within the industry. The more you know about your industry, the better you will be able to spot the rising stars that might need help from a seasoned veteran who has experience—like you! You will know what companies would be great to work for and which ones to avoid because they are faltering or have poor senior leadership. Attending industry conferences is a great place to learn what is going on and to build relationships. Everything in business is built on relationships, and the more you have, the better off you are. These are people you should work to help and provide value to when they need

Everything in business is built on relationships, and the more you have, the better off you are.

it. In turn, when you need advice or assistance they will be there to support you. I cannot emphasize this enough. If you are not networking and attending industry conferences, you are missing out on a huge opportunity for your career, especially for those looking to make a pivot to something new. These networks and connections will help you to become a rock star in your current company as you lead projects and create value for your company. When the time comes for you to explore other opportunities by pivoting into a new role within the industry, these contacts will be your best asset.

Finally, to see the bigger picture and to connect the dots, you need to have margin in your life to *learn from multiple viewpoints.*

I religiously read the *Wall Street Journal* every morning to give me a global context of things happening around the world and here in the United States. I want to see the macro picture on all things political, economic, and social, and I always try to tie it back to my industry, or business. How will this impact me? How will this impact my company? Where are the opportunities? Where are the threats? I also try to review industry periodicals, and since technology is impacting every aspect of life, I want to keep my finger on the pulse of that sector by reading TechCrunch.com (which we already mentioned) and other tech journals, looking for developments that will impact my industry. It is imperative to stay current and have a basic understanding of the global issues and currents that are shaping the world around us.

Over time it can be easy to build a bubble where we go to the same places, read news from the same websites, socialize with people who come from the same socioeconomic backgrounds, share the same religion and worldview, and in doing so we create an environment that hinders our growth and understanding of the world. It is imperative to break free from these bubbles and cultivate what Astro Teller calls "Cognitive Diversity," where we engage and get along with people who think and see the world differently from the way we do. To stay sharp and in tune with the thoughts of the day and issues that are important to multiple ethnic and religious backgrounds, I actively seek out information from a wide variety of sources and engage in friendships that will expose me to different lifestyles and worldviews.

Diversity is a beautiful element of life, and I am a firm believer that we can learn something from everyone we meet. I recommend not getting all your news from US news organizations that can have myopic worldviews and many times do not highlight other thoughts and views on subjects. I read the *London Financial Times* and the *Economist* to get a more global perspective on the news and highly recommend both. I have friends who will only watch Fox News or read the *Huffington Post* and will not have anything to do with the other. I read both because I want to see what both sides are saying, not so I can understand what our differences are but so I can understand where our common ground is.

When I mention the importance of reading and continued education I am reminded of Proverbs 3:13–14, which says, "Blessed are those who find wisdom, those who gain understanding, for she is more profitable than silver and yields better returns that gold." I often hear people say, "Bob, I would love to stay informed, read, and get more education but I am just too busy. Where do you find the time?" The answer is, I make time because I understand how important it is for me to be good at my role. I am the president of a company and father of six children and very involved in my community. There are areas of life where I will sacrifice, but this is not one. I know that to stay at the top of my game, to help my company grow,

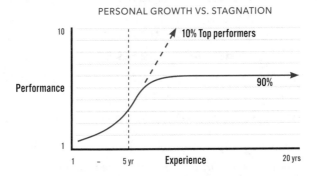

PERSONAL GROWTH VS. STAGNATION

and to stay ahead of all the changes, I need to stay current and sharp.

Over time most people will settle into a status quo, but top performers always look for ways to grow. As I said, I believe we can learn from everyone we meet. I am convinced that we as a nation need less divisiveness. Those who seek to divide do so for power and money. That is a topic for another book. I have come to learn that no matter our cultural or religious beliefs, as a people we generally have far more in common that should pull us together than we have differences that pull us apart. I have been privileged to participate in YPO forums with global leaders who hail from every corner of the globe, representing every background, religion, and worldview imaginable. The most thought-provoking, meaningful, and life-changing discussions I have had are with friends around a table at Harvard Business School who were Jewish, Muslim, Christian, atheist, and secularist. In a spirit of mutual respect and dialogue they shared beliefs, life experiences, and the way they see economic, political, and religious issues. Even in diverse settings such as this there is always much more common ground than differences, and only through respect and dialogue can we as a people learn, live together, and tackle the challenges we face. Ensure your reading and learning is broad and all-encompassing to understand the full range of complex issues that easily get glossed over in mainstream media.

EMOTIONAL INTELLIGENCE: THE "SOFT SKILLS"

"Human beings, by changing the inner attitudes of their minds, can change the outer aspects of their lives."

—WILLIAM JAMES, *American philosopher and psychologist*

In 1995 psychologist Daniel Goleman, PhD, published *Emotional Intelligence: Why It Can Matter More Than IQ*. It quickly gained critical acclaim, changing the entire landscape in the field of psychology. The *Harvard Business Review* said it was "a revolutionary, paradigm-shattering idea,"[6] while *Time* magazine named it one of the "25 Most Influential Business Management Books."[7] A few years later Goleman wrote *Primal Leadership: Realizing the Power of Emotional Intelligence* (2002). Along with *The Emotional Intelligence Quick Book* by Travis Bradberry and Jean Greaves, these three titles have become some of the books I most recommend to friends and colleagues and those I mentor. To put it simply, they are career changing. Business leaders around the globe have come to realize that skills and concepts can often be taught, but people

People without personal and group emotional intelligence are a liability, no matter how bright they are.

with poor emotional intelligence who cannot control themselves, relate to others, have situational awareness of others' feelings and needs, and are unable to work well with others are a detriment to a team and organization. Now more than ever, in highly collaborative environments where teams must work together across cultures and countries and multiple time zones, sharing information and working toward a common goal, people without personal and group

CYCLE OF TEAM BUILDING

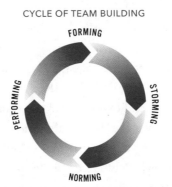

The Forming, Storming, Norming, and Performing model was developed by Bruce Tuckman.

emotional intelligence are a liability, no matter how bright they are. I have worked with people with extremely high IQs who have been praised for their industry knowledge, ability to work harder than anyone on the team, and vision for the future. Their Achilles heel, however, is low emotional intelligence, which led to constant personal issues at work, broken relationships, misunderstandings, and a trail of devastation hidden by good results. These symptoms can be overlooked for a while, but sooner or later they catch up with a person unwilling to change and make progress. Organizations starving for results might turn a blind eye to their core values and this type of behavior, but only to their long-term detriment. Organizations that have a strong moral compass will address this head-on and take action to protect their people and their culture.

Whereas some traits for success are hardwired into our DNA, this is one where anyone can become an expert. At 6'3" and 175 pounds, I never had it in me to be an NBA center. It just wasn't in my genes. Thankfully, genes do not dictate one of the most important career skills we need to master. Each one of us can vastly improve in the area of Emotional Intelligence by being dedicated to learn and grow in this area of our lives.

To get started, I highly recommend reading the two books I just mentioned. If the top CEOs and thought leaders in industry are saying that a better predictor of your success is EQ not IQ, then it should inspire everyone to learn what they are talking about and how to improve in that critical area. Emotional intelligence boils down to self-control, empathy for others, learning to place our needs and desires second to others and team goals. As Christians, we are taught to display the "fruit of the Spirit" as the apostle Paul wrote to the Galatians, summing up nine qualities that a Christian should display, saying, "But the fruit of the Spirit is love, joy, peace, forbearance, kindness, goodness, faithfulness, gentleness and self-control" (Galatians 5:22–23).

Many of these traits run counter to a me-centric, self-serving, winner-take-all attitude that many times is displayed in the culture around us. We all have known people who display narcissistic attributes that are polar opposites of the fruit of the Spirit. We have witnessed and experienced the cancerous, toxic environments such narcissism can create in families and organizations.

Most major world religions also teach against this narcissism and embrace attitudes similar to the fruit of the Spirit. Whether you are a Christian or not, we can all agree that if everyone in the world worked hard to continuously live out the fruit of the Spirit, the world would be a better place. In today's economy, where there are more applicants than there are jobs and the stress is high in many organizations, having strong emotional intelligence is critical in getting and keeping a job. No matter where you go, there will be tough issues and difficult people to deal with. I've seen it all in my career, but I have never yet found a utopian environment! The funny thing is that many people believe such idyllic environments exist in the nonprofit world, yet the reality is that very often, things are just as bad there as in the government and private sector, and for all the same reasons. The longer you go in your career and the further you rise in corporate ranks with more responsibility and stress, the more essential emotional intelligence will be to your success—and the lack thereof will play a major part in your downfall.

All of us have blind spots, and the higher we climb in the corporate ranks, the more obvious those blind spots become to others and less to ourselves.

However, it's not just about success but our health as well. Travis Bradberry and Jean Greaves in their book *The Emotional Intelligence Quick Book* highlight the following:

> The physical impact of emotional intelligence is so strong that studies at Harvard Medical School have actually mapped physical difference in the brain based on changes in emotional intelligence. In these studies, the amount of "traffic" flowing between the rational and emotional

centers of the brain was found to have real impact on their size and structure. Emotional intelligence skills strengthen your brain's ability to cope with emotional distress. This resilience keeps your immune systems strong and helps protect you from disease.[8]

To gain a starting point and understanding of where you are, I am a big fan of the emotional intelligence assessment offered by Travis Bradberry and Jean Greaves at www.TalentSmart.com. This will give you a good baseline of your strengths and weaknesses and how to improve in this area of your career. All of us have blind spots, and the higher we climb in the corporate ranks, the more obvious those blind spots become to others and less to ourselves. People who report to you will not risk angering or alienating a boss for fear of career blowback, but they are the ones who see and experience our blind spots daily. We need to get that feedback so we can improve; and we need to create an environment and culture where people can safely and constructively give that feedback. I have found systems that allow for anonymous feedback are the best because people will be more open.

I once had a boss who said, "Bob, we are partners in this thing together. I need you to help hold me accountable and let me know if you see blind spots or issues that I need to fix." Thinking he was being serious and a person who wanted to improve, I took him up on it. About a year later I noticed some things happening in his personal life that were impacting the business and how he treated staff members. I brought it up with him, trying to help as a friend. Instantly the relationship changed and a passive-aggressive environment developed. He was okay with me publicly praising him, but this constructive criticism from a friend he could not handle. I learned a big lesson that day, one that most people in the corporate ranks know: what most people say and what they want is totally different. Your relationship with your boss is as critical as your job performance, and most leaders can't take honest feedback and criticism, so be careful before you offer that criticism. Even if they ask for it.

Because of this, those of us who want real honest feedback need to create a culture to get it. Luckily, receiving feedback from those up the chain of command is easy. What we need is feedback from both our peers and those who work for us. Great leaders and supervisors create environments where it is safe for those around them to give feedback. A formal instrument like a 360-degree review is a great place to start. Ask your Human Resources Department (HR) or your direct supervisor if you can get a 360-degree feedback this year as part of your performance report, because you want to find out the areas you need to improve. Most people are terrified of these types of reports and would rather live in complacent denial. Requesting this report will show that you are secure in yourself with high EQ and are committed to learning, growing, and becoming a better team member for the organization. It will send a powerful message to your supervisor.

Growing in our EQ is important. We are called to strive to grow daily in living out the fruit of the Spirit. I often fall short, but that is my goal. When we demonstrate love, kindness, faithfulness, and self-control to our fellow humans, we not only inspire others to do the same, but also we make the world a better place and live a life with less drama, a life full of richness knowing we are helping others and ourselves at the same time. Don't do it solely for your career—but as a by-product you will see your career and opportunities for leadership grow. Success is a natural outcome of developing and mastering this area of your life.

A final key for success is to learn to see the world through different lenses. This requires immense self-awareness and situational perception. Once you can see the world through the eyes of those

CYCLE OF SELF-AWARENESS

you work with, you can develop *empathy* for their needs and concerns. The absolute worst people I have worked with did not have the ability to see others' points of view. Being blind to this is just as bad as knowing the truth but not caring.

Once you acquire this ability to see the world through the eyes of those around you and to have empathy for them, you will have mastered emotional intelligence. Throughout your career, work to replace ego with empathy, and you will not only be successful but loved, respected, and remembered for the impact you had on the lives around you.

COMMUNICATION: STORYTELLING, MOTIVATING, INFLUENCING

"Words are, of course, the most powerful drug used by mankind."—RUDYARD KIPLING

One theme I hope you are grasping thus far is that the more challenging way is almost always the right way. The path that is difficult and requires work and practice is usually the better choice because so many people are okay with average and won't do the extra work to achieve those skills. Therefore, you actually have less competition and a higher probability for success.

Talking about "the path that is difficult," ask almost any business or professional person, from anywhere on the globe, what their greatest fear is, and they will probably list public speaking at or near the top of the list. Whether you are a novice, terrified of being called upon to give a speech, or a seasoned veteran who loves getting in front of a large audience, we all can remember the fear of our first time. The cold sweaty hands, the heart beating out of our chest, worrying we would trip walking to the mic, losing our train of thought, worried our fly was open (Fun Fact: I have perfected the art of acting like I am straightening my tie or tucking in my shirt to make sure it is still up). Communicating is critical to your success, and mastering this art can supercharge your career. Demonstrating this ability will not only give you greater opportunity at your current company, but it will also help you when you interview for your next job, not to mention affording you greater opportunities later in your career. I have witnessed talented senior leaders who can run an effective meeting in a small group of close personal contacts, but when called upon to present an idea in a board meeting or make a presentation in front of a crowd, they blow it. It really becomes their Achilles heel when they're seeking new roles and opportunities. Don't be that person!

It is important for us to be able to communicate to others in both written and oral form. For those who really want to master this area I highly recommend Dr. Frank Luntz's book *Words That Work: It's Not What You Say, It's What People Hear*. It will help you with emails, meetings, speeches, and marketing for your company. You have probably seen Dr. Luntz on Fox News and CNN, providing insight on what politicians are saying and how they are crafting their messages for the public. Here is a short synopsis:

> This book is about the art and science of words that work. Examining the strategic and tactical use of language in politics, business, and

everyday life, it shows you how you can achieve better results by narrowing the gap between what you intend to convey and what your audiences actually interpret . . . look at the world from your listener's point of view. In essence, it is listener centered.[9]

What we say to others is as important as what we say to ourselves. I won't go too far into this subject as I covered it more in depth in my first book, *The Leap: Launching Your Full-Time Career in Our Part-Time Economy*. However, it is important to remind readers of Proverbs 18:21, "The tongue has the power of life and death, and those who love it will eat its fruit." Just as our words have power and meaning with our children and others around us and can inspire them to greatness or tear them down in defeat, what we say to ourselves has the same impact.

Most people do not have an issue talking about things they are passionate about and have deep expertise on. Actually, the problem is getting them to stop! The key is to apply that passion and that expertise to the areas where we will have to communicate with others.

Whether preparing for a speech, a business meeting, a sales pitch, or closing a deal, I always follow these six steps:

1. Be prepared—practice, and never try to wing it.
2. Know the subject matter—become an expert on the topic.
3. What is the objective? Have a clear goal; otherwise you're wasting your time and theirs.
4. Share data—Some people just want the big story; others only want data. Give both!
5. What are the most likely questions? Be prepared to answer them with facts.
6. You don't need to have all the answers. It's okay to say, "I don't know but I will find out for you." People appreciate honesty and transparency.

In our careers we will need to communicate to influence both up and down the chain of command. It is an art to both "influence up" to get budgets or projects approved, or "influence down" to get teams to rally around a cause, work longer hours, or deliver a major project on time.

The art is once again putting yourself in the listeners' position (remember our discussion of empathy?) and understanding their needs and wants, and showing them how these needs will be met, based on them following your plan.

It is up to you to connect the dots. Connect them and you will get what you need. Don't and you won't. It is as easy as that. Everyone is self-interested to some degree, and communicating to influence inside or outside your company needs to satisfy that self-interest. Communicating to motivate is no different.

Those who can effectively communicate orally and with the written word will be effective in leading meetings, closing deals, motivating employees, influencing outside leaders, and building industry partnerships. These types of communicators build influence throughout industries and display confidence and competency in their duties. Since few people are polished communicators and influencers, it is easy to set yourself apart from the crowd with just a little practice.

BECOME A LIFELONG LEARNER: ACQUIRING NEW SKILLS

"Adapt to the future and invest in yourself, no matter how comfortable you are with your career!"—ERIKA FRY, *Fortune* magazine

"The skill of learning things quickly . . . [is] critical for the rest of your life," proclaimed Astro Teller to the students at Stanford University. Shortly before, in the same talk, this Silicon Valley innovator had told his audience that everything they were learning at one of the most prestigious universities in the world would be irrelevant in ten years.[10] With the exception of this one critical skill.

Time and time again as I speak with college administrators, company executives, and hiring professionals I hear them say that one of the most significant benefits of a college education is not necessarily the knowledge that one obtains there but the ability to quickly tackle new subjects and skills and add them to your tool belt for future use. "Learning how to learn" in college is, in many respects, more important than your degree. A Harvard Business School professor with thirty years of tenure told me that the standard undergraduate degree has a shelf life of three years today, and that students need to continue on their education journey postgraduation, acquiring new skills and staying current both in their industry and in technological advancements that might disrupt that industry.

> **"Learning how to learn" in college is, in many respects, more important than your degree.**

The professor's comment follows the advice of IBM CEO Ginni Rometty, who says, "Always disrupt yourself."[11] This is a much better position to be in than the person who has their head in the sand, fails to take proactive steps in their career, helplessly watches the world change around them, and wakes up one morning jobless and irrelevant. As four-star Army General Eric Shinseki says, "If you don't like change you will like irrelevance even less."[12] So how do we become lifelong learners, continuing to add skills and disrupting ourselves so we are prepared for the next economy shift? It is easier now than ever.

Before we get started, let me address the big question everyone will have: *Do I have the time?* At first glance you and I will say no. We are overscheduled and overcommitted, and we will ask ourselves how in the world we will find time to start learning and adding new skills. Author and social media expert Gary Vaynerchuk wrote an article that asked people to audit their 7:00 p.m. to 2:00 a.m. time. It is a fantastic post, showing that most of us have all sorts of time available to leverage for learning and launching new projects—but we just need to prioritize better.[13]

A mentor of mine used to say often, "Bob, you will earn a living from nine to five but earn your fortune after 5:00 p.m." In essence, to achieve anything in life, we need to be willing to put in the time. So if you want to learn new skills, you will have to carve out consistent time each day, dedicating yourself to this pursuit. There is no shortcut, no easy way around it. It's hard—which is the reason that if you pursue this direction, *you* will have success because so many people will be unwilling to make the sacrifice and will settle for being content with average. You will find success because few will take the path with you.

Where you start

You are already ahead of your peers in this endeavor since you have picked up the habit of staying current with global news and economic trends—as we have already discussed. Now, to further this self-education, I recommend reading books. You might think, "Now that isn't surprising, coming from an author!" but I want you to see the bigger picture. According to a 2015 Pew report, 27 percent of Americans did not read a book in the last year, with the median being four books read in a year. I want you to be firmly ahead of that group of Americans.[14] By being dedicated and intentional with the knowledge you will acquire in your spare time, you will be competing with only 46 percent of Americans, of whom 28 percent are readers who read eleven or more books a year. *This* is the group you want to be in. As John Maxwell has famously said, "Leaders are readers!" and time and time again we see the most successful in society, those who are making waves and at the forefront of change, are voracious readers. I consistently see the wisest and most effective people in life as committed lifelong learners who, regardless of time constraints, are dedicated to reading. Reading one book a month is possible, and lack of time is not an excuse. If US presidents, along with the likes of Bill Gates, Steve Jobs, Carly Fiorina, and other industry leaders, consistently take time to read with their busy schedules, everyone can. I recommend reading books on leaders and on subjects that will give breadth and depth to your current skill set. My goal is to average two books a month throughout the year. Here are a few of my favorites for 2015.

1. *40/40 Vision*
2. *Abundance*
3. *Team of Teams*
4. *Losing the Signal*
5. *The End of Power*
6. *A Whole New Mind*
7. *The Talent Code*
8. *The Hard Thing About Hard Things*
9. *Smart Cuts*
10. *5 Gears*

How can reading impact you? In his book *Power*, author Jeffrey Pfeffer tells a story about Joe Beneducci, Chief Operating Officer of Fireman's Fund, a $12 billion division of Allianz. At the young age of thirty-nine he was recognized as one of the top tech-savvy executives of the year. When asked how he could achieve such a great honor at such a young age, he said that he had an average academic background but was committed to reading one nonfiction book a week to gain knowledge and self-development. This is the secret of all high achievers I have met, and something that everyone can easily implement in their life.

The obvious way to add skills and competencies is to go back to college to get a degree or an advanced degree. Should you? This all depends on your goals. I know one successful entrepreneur who has an undergraduate degree, along with law and MBA degrees from a top state university, and is going back to get an Executive MBA from Wharton Business School because he knows this will help his career and his long-term objectives. Your goals may not require you to go back to get another degree. It is also important to note that adding education without a plan on how you intend to leverage it is a mistake. Many students have blindly added $100,000 or more of student loan debt to obtain degrees they can't use or are not valuable in the job market. Starting with a plan can help you avoid those mistakes. Not all education or degrees are equal. If you are going to pay for an education, make sure you have a good ROI (Return on Investment) and that your earning potential increases after your graduation.

Skills: the big three

If you aren't sure what skills would be helpful in your career, I would encourage you to think about adding skills to your résumé in one of three areas:

1. Foreign language
2. Technology (coding)
3. General Business (MBA courses via MOOCs)

I firmly believe that everyone should have some general proficiency in these areas, and it is easier than ever to add these skills to your tool belt, and you can do it for free or almost free.

In our global economy where everything is connected and the world continues to get smaller, those who speak English have a massive advantage, because it is becoming the universal language of business. However, this does not mean English speakers should not master a second language. The easiest to learn are Spanish, French, Portuguese, and Italian. To become proficient in these, it is estimated that it could take 575 to 600 class hours of study. The hardest are Arabic and Mandarin, which, it is estimated, take about 2,200 class hours of study to master.[15]

Of course, the hardest will present more opportunities. As a side note, my oldest daughter is taking Mandarin, and it has surprisingly become her favorite subject. I'm going to encourage my other children to take it as well. I highly recommend Rosetta Stone as a method for learning a second language. The average cost for the course is less than $200 to get started. Those in military and government service who need to learn a language quickly often use this method.

> **Coding is nothing more than problem solving and using computer languages to do it.**

Coding is nothing more than problem solving and using computer languages to do it. I hope by now that everyone is 100 percent clued in to the fact that technology is changing everything, globally and rapidly. Those who have an understanding of the basics of technology, can speak the language, and can leverage key concepts, can have a huge edge in this new economy. If you want to add tech skills to your résumé, you don't have to go back to college and get a four-year degree in computer science. Multiple professionals I have mentored over the past year have started adding this skill to their résumé by taking free online courses through CodeAcademy.com. Others leverage KhanAcademy.org, which is completely free and gives a great intro into programming or coding.

Currently, many believe the best language to learn is Javascript. With a basic understanding and proficiency, you can move on to

HTML, Ruby on Rails, and Python, considered by many to be the easiest language to learn.

In the realm of technology, it is truly a meritocracy. Companies do not care where you went to school or what degree you have. All they care about is that you can do the job. There are so few people with these skill sets that those who possess them, many taught from home leveraging platforms like Code Academy, Khan Academy, Tree House, and Udacity, are able to totally dictate the terms of their employment. One headhunter in Nashville said that the unemployment rate for people with this type of training is 0.3 percent, and that those with average skills are garnering $100,000-plus starting salary offers from companies desperate for their help. If you are in a dying industry, frustrated with your future prospects, or looking for a big change, you must check this out. It is the modern-day gold rush, and you can learn the skills from home after work each night.

I was recently flying home from Seattle and sat next to a young man who was feverishly coding on his computer. Amazed at what he was doing, I interrupted him and started asking a few questions. Yes, I was one of those annoying guys who you always hope doesn't sit beside you on your next flight! I learned he was graduating in the spring from Duke University with a degree in Computer Science and was returning from interviews with Microsoft, Amazon, Google, and Facebook. I asked him about the interview process for each and what he learned through the experience. I was curious as to whether having a Duke degree helped him get in the door. He said his Duke credentials might have helped, but it was all about whether he could problem-solve and code. "That is really what they care about." He said they would put him in front of a whiteboard, give him a problem, and watch him solve it. They also analyzed all the code he had been working on and posting on his Github.com account. "Either you can code or you can't. It is right there for everyone to see. They want to see how you think and how you problem-solve. It truly is a meritocracy in the technology world." He accepted a job at Google and is now programming for them!

For general education courses, look into Massive Open Online Courses (MOOCs). These platforms are revolutionizing and democratizing education for the masses, allowing people all over the world to take the same courses from top global institutions like Harvard, MIT, Yale, Stanford, Michigan, Virginia, Georgia Tech, and others via the Internet. Sites like EdX, Udemy, Coursera, and Udacity will give you free access for thousands of courses in all subject matters, including accounting, finance, history, computer programming, design, physics, engineering, and many more. The courses are generally free but sometimes cost a nominal fee of $25–$60 per course to receive official certification that you took and passed the course. Many people are taking these courses and adding them to their official résumés and LinkedIn accounts to demonstrate newly acquired skills and that they are on a continual self-development pathway in their career.

Since this is a new certification process that is changing higher education, I wrote a free eBook to help people understand how to add these certifications to their résumé and how to discuss this education in their interviews with prospective employers who may not be familiar with MOOCs. You can download it at this link: www.RobertDickie.com.

Finally, whether you are thinking of pivoting into your own start-up business or into another job in your industry or different career field altogether, a sound understanding of the principles of business is critical for both entrepreneurial success and advancement in corporate America. The Master of Business Administration, or MBA, has been the advanced degree of choice for those in the business world. Depending on where you go, this two-year degree can range from $60,000 to well over $186,000 for the most prestigious schools like Harvard and Wharton. Those who have MBA training and desirable skill sets under their belt set themselves apart from their peers and make themselves much more marketable. If you don't have two years or the money to invest in a full-time MBA program, consider getting the skills, education, and certification for free by using the MOOC method previously mentioned; your entire program can be tailored at NoPayMBA.com.

Laurie Pickard is the creator and founder of NoPayMBA, which has been highlighted in the *Wall Street Journal, London Financial Times, Forbes, Entrepreneur,* and other media outlets around the world. As an aid worker in Africa who wanted to get an MBA but could not due to her location, she developed an entire MBA program, leveraging the best curricula from the top business schools around the world to get an MBA equivalent for less than $1,000, all while studying and completing work in Africa. You can do this from anywhere in the world. Her program is amazing, and I highly recommend it. Whether you are setting out to be an entrepreneur or pivoting to scale the corporate ladder, this MBA equivalent designation on your résumé will help you stand out from your peers. More importantly, the knowledge and skills that you will acquire from this program and how you acquired it through leveraging new technology is the type of self-disruption and improvement we all need to be pursuing in our careers.

CHARACTER AND INTEGRITY

"Knowledge will give you power, but character respect."
—BRUCE LEE

A principle that I have learned states that "money and opportunity always flow to trust." This principle works both in global macroeconomic terms and at the individual level. Look at countries around the world torn by lawlessness, malfeasance, and a breakdown of trust and accountability and you will see that global companies exit en masse. Foreign Direct Investment (FDI) declines as investors pull money out of the untrustworthy system, looking for a place with sound laws and a trustworthy system where they can safely invest. Countries like Zimbabwe, Venezuela, and Afghanistan with unstable governments, lax laws, and war and unrest rank at the bottom of the list for FDI, while the United States is still the largest receiver of FDI and is seen as the safe haven of choice for foreign investors and governments looking to park capital long term.[16] The United Kingdom and Hong Kong follow closely behind.

Economies that are undergirded by strong laws, sound governance, and anti-corruption policies always receive the greatest investments. The same is true for people. Character and integrity are everything in business and in life.

As I have lectured around the country, I tell college students that I always hire for character and integrity first, then competence and loyalty. I learned this from mentors and from firsthand experience. Whether business partners or staff members, it does not matter how smart and talented someone is. If they have poor character, the relationship will always end in trouble. The drama and hassle are just not worth it. You can teach skill sets and give new members of the team on-the-job training in critical areas of the operation, but if they lack character and integrity, your teaching will go only so far.

I have worked with executives around the world from all faith backgrounds and cultures from every corner of the globe. Finding talented people that have character and integrity is of utmost importance to them.

Always protect and continue to develop your character. It takes a lifetime to build a reputation and only a second to destroy it. We have seen examples of public leaders who took shortcuts to success and broke the public's trust, and they will never be able to earn it back. Your character and integrity will follow you, and through interviewing friends and business associates, prospective employers will be trying to ascertain whether you are a person that can be counted on. Like the story of Joseph in the Bible, no matter the cost, always remain faithful protecting your integrity, and you will be rewarded. The most highly sought-after commodity in any nation around the world is a man or woman with a strong moral compass who can be trusted to do the right thing. Be known as that person and you will always find opportunities when you pivot. The Bible is full of examples of people who faced challenges and pivoted in life and maintained their character like Joseph, Daniel, and Jonathan.

> ➤ PIVOT POINTS Lifelong Learning

I hope by now you are convinced of the importance of becoming a lifelong learner. Here are some easy steps to start taking today to add skills to your résumé. Whether you are young and fresh out of college or late in your career looking for ways to extend your career or pivot into something new, we all need to be adding new skills.

MOOCs (Massive Open Online Courses)—These are the most reputable MOOC providers that I recommend.

1. EdX.org
2. Coursera.org
3. Udacity.org
4. NoPayMBA.com—This site is for those who want to get an MBA through leveraging MOOCs.

Nanodegrees—This is one of the best ways to gain specific knowledge quickly that can be leveraged in the workforce.

Companies like Google are sponsoring these programs and monitoring the progress of students taking courses that they deem critical for their success. Top-performing students in these programs are being recruited and offered jobs by Google and others! This is incredible. You can gain useful knowledge for your career and at the same time, based on your performance, can get on the radar to be recruited by some of the top global companies. These are some Nanodegree programs I would look into. These are all offered at Udacity.org.

1. Android Basics Nanodegree—by Google
2. Machine Learning Engineer—by Google
3. Intro to Programming Nanodegree
4. Front End Web Developer Nanodegree
5. Data Analyst Nanodegree
6. Intro to Data Analysis
7. How to Build a Start-up
8. Product Design
9. Introduction to Data Science—Washington University
10. Data Science—Johns Hopkins University

Audible.com—I have an Audible account and supplement my education with audiobooks. This is a great way to take travel and commute times, along with other downtime in our schedules, and make them useful. With this I am able to add at least one more book per month that I would not otherwise have time to read. This is the best app I have found for audiobooks. I like physical books over audiobooks because I take notes in them for future reference, but to take notes with Audible I just tap the "clip" button on the app when I hear a segment I want to save for the future. This will save the last thirty seconds of the book. At the end of the book you can go back and access all your "clips." I use Evernote.com to keep track of my notes and will open a new note for each book and will go back and add notes from all my "clips" so I can access these on the fly, in meetings, or when I need to quickly recall a fact.

Certifications—There are many types of certifications you can receive that can help you in your career. Three of the top-paying certifications in 2016:

1. Amazon Web Services Certified Solutions Architect—$125,000
2. PMP (Project Management Professional)—$116,000
3. Six Sigma Green Belt—$102,000

Many times a company will pay for staff members to get specialized certifications that will help them in their job. A new certification that is growing in popularity is SCRUM certification. This is a new method of project development/management that is taking the economy by storm because it is used widely with great results in the tech sector. I recently became SCRUM Master Certified and strongly recommend this certification. A three-day course might cost $1,200, and there are multiple additional trainings and certifications that you can add on top of this over time. Investigate whether there are certifications you can acquire that will help you in your job.

MAKE IT HAPPEN

"Belief in oneself is incredibly infectious. It generates momentum, the collective force of which far outweighs any kernel of self-doubt that might creep in."

AIMEE MULLINS, *athlete, actress, Paralympics champion*

A cold wind swept through the streets of Washington, D.C., freezing the spectators who stood on the sidewalks cheering the thousands of runners in the 2002 Marine Corps Marathon. I was supposed to be challenging for the victory, but that possibility was fading fast, faster than my slowing pace in the latter stages of this, my first marathon. I felt the wind's presence as I ran into a headwind, fighting against me, forcing me to exert extra effort with every step. After miles of physical exhaustion, my uniform wet with sweat, I was dehydrated and becoming hypothermic. I had been in contention early on and things were going according to plan, but then the "wheels came off," as my coach would later say.

He couldn't understand it. I was in perfect position at eighteen miles to start my long drive to the finish line of this grueling

26.2-mile race. This is what we had trained so hard for. We had planned on everything—but not this. Not a disaster unfolding just a few miles from the finish line. As I slowed down, cramping in pain, laboring with every step, the eventual victor and lead pack pulled ahead and slowly vanished from sight. I was now a mere participant just hoping to finish, and even that was in question. As I rounded a turn near the Pentagon just a mile from the finish line, a vision burned into my memory that I will never forget. Two ladies standing on the sidewalk looked at me running—well, slowly jogging—toward them, and one lady turned to the other and said, "I don't think he's going to make it!"

Within a few yards of that spot I felt a sharp pain in my Achilles tendon like someone had shot me, and I fell to the pavement in pain. Crawling to the edge of the road, I removed myself from the race and sat in the gutter of the street just a short distance from the Marine Corps Memorial and the finish line I would never cross that day. Shivering in the cold, I found a discarded and soot-covered white ladies' fleece that had been left from the start earlier in the day. I wrapped it around my cold body to stay warm as I sat there waiting for help. I also found a half-eaten PowerBar still in the wrapper. So hungry without any thought of whose it might have been, I ate the remainder like it was my last meal. Soon, two Marines came and helped me back to the finish line and to the medical tent, where I received treatment and my coach met me.

What a day. What a disappointment. I was not expecting this, and I had no one to blame but myself.

A year earlier my close friend Gary Brimmer, a member of the United States Army stationed with me in Hawaii, had convinced me to start training for a marathon. I had been a track and cross-country runner at the University of Tennessee, and he felt that I could transition to the marathon and have success. He introduced me to his coach in Hawaii, who soon became mine as well. Farley Simon was a Marine and had earned fame in the Corps by being the first Marine to win the storied and prestigious Marine Corps Marathon in Washington, D.C. The Marine Corps Marathon also serves as an interservice competition among all branches of the US military, which send teams to compete against each other for bragging rights. Gary was on the Army team and I would soon be on the Air Force team, with Farley training us both. Farley, the masterful coach, knew exactly what it would take to run this marathon and do well. We formulated a plan for success that would require months of build-up, long morning runs, twenty-plus-mile runs each weekend, countless track workouts for speed, and training in the weight room to prepare our bodies for the abuse it would have to endure over 26.2 miles.

As a former college athlete at the University of Tennessee, I had trained with some of the best athletes in the world. Multiple teammates had made the US Olympic team. I had been captain of both the track and cross-country teams my senior year and fared well in my career, earning All-SEC honors and setting a track record in the 3,000m. I was confident I knew what I was doing.

You know that old saying about "pride goes before a fall"? I was about to experience that in a very real way.

As the months progressed, Farley would check in with me each week on my progress as some of my runs and workouts were conducted on my own. My reports were always positive. My body was holding up and I was getting stronger. However, I failed to realize how devastating minor alterations to the plan might be, so I failed to mention these tweaks to Farley. Instead of following the plan 100 percent as it had been drawn up by my coach, the guy who knew what it took to win because he had done it twice, I started to make minor adjustments. It wasn't anything major, mind you. A long weekend run might call for eighteen miles, and I might push it a bit farther, going twenty-two and harder than prescribed. Sometimes I would tailor a workout doing something I had done at UT. After all, I was a college athlete and knew how to train, and I felt confident in my abilities and knowledge of the sport.

I knew what the problem was. I hadn't listened to my coach.

As the race neared, Farley checked my progress, my times, and the work he had prescribed for me to do. Knowing the entrants in the field, he started to surmise that not only would I most likely be in the lead pack from the start of the race, but that I might have a chance to win. I could be the first Air Force runner to win this race! It was a big deal, and we started to get excited. Leaders at Hickam AFB knew of my goal, and the community rallied behind me. Upon arriving in DC, Farley and I attended the pre-race convention, and he started introducing me to other runners and his friends as the Air Force guy who had a chance to win. The pressure was mounting.

Now Farley stood next to me in the medical tent, doing his best to console me. He knew I was injured and beyond disappointed. My family had flown in to watch the race and were worried when I never crossed the line. Although I was in pain, the biggest pain was that of embarrassment, knowing I was returning home as a DNF—"Did Not Finish."

Farley said we would connect back in Hawaii. On the way home, I had a lot to think about. I knew what the problem was. I hadn't listened to my coach. I got in the way and started coming up with my own plans, thinking I could take things I learned at UT and add them to the system to make the plan better. Big mistake. Now I was facing the consequences of my decision.

As you can imagine, I received a good deal of good-natured

ribbing and teasing from fellow officers in my unit about the disaster. On my first morning back to work, some of the staff wore brown paper bags over their heads at their desks with the eyes cut out, like you see at games of NFL teams that have terrible records for the season. It was funny, but at the same time I felt humiliated. This was a pretty big and public failure on my part. I told Farley what happened and promised him if he would coach me again for another race I would follow his plan 100 percent and would not deviate from it. The great guy he is, it did not take long at all for him to start drawing up another plan, and this time I would listen and execute!

"FALL SEVEN . . . RISE EIGHT."
—Japanese Proverb

The goal was to enter the Boston Marathon in the spring of 2003, just seven months away. Farley pulled strings and got me an "elite athlete" entry into the field of upwards of 30,000 runners. I would be starting right up front with the best runners in the world. I was just DNF in my first marathon and now my coach was going to put me on the starting line of arguably the most storied and prestigious marathon in the world, with the best runners in the world. He looked at me and said, "Bob, I believe in you. If you do exactly as I say, you will run well and surprise yourself and everyone else!"

This was redemption time for me. I trained like a madman with the memories of my past failure motivating me every day. I was never more driven in my life. I could not wait to step to that line. Every minute of every day that race consumed me. While working I had reminders of that race on my desk. After work, I was training. I was 100 percent dedicated to our goal, and I was not going to let my coach or family down again. After all, many people were making sacrifices on this journey with me.

On April 21, 2003, I stepped to the starting line of the Boston

Marathon, knowing I was prepared. I had followed my coach's plan 100 percent, no deviations. I had worked harder than ever before in my life. I was nervous and excited, but there was no pressure. I knew I was ready. As tens of thousands of spectators lined the course that day, I ran with pride, wearing my Air Force uniform. As I ran by, the crowd would erupt in chants of "U-S-A!" I was running with the best from around the world, and the crowd was cheering me on.

The moment was so surreal. A few months before, I could not even finish a marathon, but on this day I finished twenty-third overall, the third American finisher, running 2:30:21 in my first marathon ever. I didn't set an American record or qualify for the Olympics, but for me it was a huge victory. I proved something to myself and to others. I had redeemed myself from a past mistake, and the joy of that moment will be something I carry with me for the rest of my life. It taught me many things, lessons that I share around the country when I give talks on this race and the principles I learned that apply to our lives and our careers.

First, face your fears

So how *do* we make our career pivots happen? How do we accomplish the dreams and goals that are before us? There is a definitive plan of action we can use, but it is impossible to get started without first talking about our fears . . . and one of the greatest fears that I see most often in others is the fear of failure. The reality is that we all have had failures in life. It comes with the territory. I certainly have had many. A mentor early in my career reminded me that we will learn more from our failures than our successes, and I have found that to be true. That was the case for me at the Marine Corps Marathon. My errors were abundantly clear during and after that horrible race, but I was able to learn a lot from it. That failure also helped give birth to one of my greatest athletic successes. The key with failure is how we classify it and the perspective we gain from that setback. Do we learn and rebound from our failures or let them become excuses that hold us back from ever trying again?

Our culture has trained us to think of failure as something to be avoided. We have a generation of children who are risk averse, fearful of trying anything new. So it is in the business world, where I have often heard the statement, "People are motivated by fear or greed." I've seen it for myself; too many people are paralyzed with irrational fears that hold them back in their career. Not wanting to change and defaulting to the easier path, they are pulled along by inertia in a predetermined direction, whether or not that direction is in alignment with their dreams and aspirations. Until the pain of the status quo is greater than the pain of change, most people will not change. It is just human nature.

What we are most afraid of almost never happens.

But we don't just struggle with the fear of failure; we also struggle with the fear of loss. This is more commonly called "loss aversion," and in the realm of economics this theory is well known and documented. People are much more strongly motivated by fear of loss than the prospect of gain. For example, a person would have a more intense emotional response to losing a thousand dollars than they would to winning that same thousand! Therefore, people become more motivated by the need to prevent loss—and more opposed to seeking out new opportunities for gain. You see where this is going. Many times this will impact us in our careers as we hold on to jobs that are unfulfilling, out of fear of losing a job and not finding another one, or fear of losing social status and positional authority that we might not otherwise attain elsewhere.

So how do we combat this fear and loss aversion and break out of the status quo, taking action to make our leap or pivot to a new opportunity? *New York Times* bestselling author Tim Ferriss said in a 2015 podcast that "we are held back by false constructs and untested assumptions."[1] What we are most afraid of almost never happens. We conjure up worst-case scenarios and dwell on them as if they were imminent, when in reality nothing could be further from the truth. A close YPO friend of mine who is a seasoned entrepreneur was launching a new business venture where almost all of his net worth was tied up in the project. He had spent his entire career going from one deal to the next in similar fashion. Once I asked him how he dealt with the pressure. He said he asks himself, "Well, what's the worst thing that could happen? I lose it all. Then what? I can always go find a job somewhere working at a department store or something. I'll be able to pay my bills and put a roof over my head. I'll find a way to take care of my family and I'll be able to leave work at 5:00 p.m. each day, have more family time and much less stress. Actually, the worst thing that can happen isn't that bad."

> **Some might say, "I'm not going to do anything. I have faith that something will happen." I consider that more a demonstration of being lazy than a sign of faith.**

It was a great way to contextualize the problem and remove all stress from his life. His worst-case scenario was pretty encouraging! More often than not, if you ask yourself what the worst-case scenario is, and you are really honest with yourself, you will find that it isn't that bad and the chance of it happening is very low!

Second, we need to overcome our fears, believe in ourselves and in our abilities, and be motivated by our God-given calling. Most importantly we need to have faith and confidence that God has a plan for us. "'For I know the plans I have for you,' declares the LORD, 'plans to prosper you and not to harm you, plans to give you hope and a future'" (Jeremiah 29:11). Wow! How awesome is that? What more could we ask for? I believe that everyone has been uniquely designed with a special plan and purpose. We are not here by accident but by design, with unique skills and talents to be used to help others and make the world a better place. When we know what our abilities are and what we were designed to do, we should not fear moving confidently in that direction, because we know God will be guiding our steps.

Living this life is an act of faith. But if we wait until a door opens or an offer comes to us, are we acting in faith? Some might say, "Well, I'm not going to do anything. I have faith something will happen." I consider that more a demonstration of being lazy than a sign of faith. I have had deep discussions with some people who have said, "Bob, I am content. I believe something will happen and I will be content until that time comes. Are you telling me not to be content?" I think this is yet another great cop-out. Once we know what God wants us to do, what we are called to do, it is imperative that we take action. God is not expecting us to be content at that point and wait for something to happen. He is expecting us to have faith and make plans and take decisive action, and through our *action* things will become clear and opportunities will arise. We are to be content but not complacent!

EYES ON THE PRIZE

As we confront and overcome our fear of failure and loss, what keeps us going? We have to have an end in mind, a goal, a prize. We have to burn with the desire to make it happen. I hope you have had a goal that burned so deeply inside of you that it consumed you as you pursued it with everything you had. If you have, then you know the type of laser focus and drive you will need as you make your career pivot. This is not a part-time, dabble-with-it-every-now-and-then exercise.

There is an old story of the philosopher Socrates, who was once approached by a young man asking him to teach him how to gain wisdom. Socrates agreed and invited the young man to follow him to a nearby pool of water. They waded in up to their chests, at which point Socrates turned to the young man, grabbing his head and forcing it underwater. Stunned, the young man waited to be released, but Socrates continued to hold his head under the water. Now panicking, the young man started to fight for survival, and finally Socrates allowed him to surface. As the young man gasped for air, bewildered by the experience, Socrates said, "You will gain wisdom when you want it as badly as your next breath of air."

The same holds true for us in our careers. For someone to make a successful pivot and change in their career, they have to want it just as badly. I have met and counseled many people who were unsatisfied in their career. Some were utterly miserable and desperate for a change. Plagued with a narcissistic boss, slave to a job that did not leverage their skill sets and without any potential for development, trapped in a toxic environment negatively impacting their health, watching the world pass them by, all the time talking about making a change to something new but always having some excuse as to why now is "not the best time." What they all didn't realize is that NOW is always the best time—it just may not be comfortable or convenient. News flash: when you are in that type of negative environment and you know you want or need to change, it will never be comfortable, but it will almost always be worth it! I have watched people talk about the need to make changes in their twenties, and year after year slips by and soon they are in their thirties or forties, still talking about it, wishing they had taken action years earlier.

Life does not get simpler with age. It gets busier and more complicated, and the longer we put off making changes the harder it becomes. Once you know you need to make a change, it is critical to start taking steps *that day* in the direction you want to go. Making a pivot to a new career or job will not happen overnight, but we can take steps daily that get us closer to our goal.

Lessons from Scrooge

Part of the process to help us develop the desire and motivation to make the needed changes in our lives comes from attaching deep emotions and feelings to those changes (or lack thereof). One exercise that has been used by many professional coaches around the world is the "Dickens Process."

We all remember the Charles Dickens novel *A Christmas Carol,* where bitter, miserly Ebenezer Scrooge is visited by three ghosts: the ghosts of Christmas past, present, and future. They show him his life from an outsider's perspective, helping him remember decisions from the past,

It is an emotional, transformative event for Scrooge to see the impact on tomorrow of inaction today.

missed opportunities in the present, and the consequences in the future. Poor Ebenezer is hardly moved by visions from the past and present, offering excuses and rationalizations for his choices and behavior and staunchly defending the life he built for himself. However, things take a different turn when he sees his future and the consequences he will reap. Ebenezer is completely undone by seeing what his future holds for him—unless he makes changes. It is an emotional, transformative event for him to see the impact on tomorrow of inaction today. Only then is he capable to make the changes needed to avoid that future pain.

We can all relate to Scrooge. Almost all of us can name changes we need to make today. Then why don't we? Because there is not a strong enough emotional driver to motivate us to do so. Through the Dickens process, a facilitator can help you imagine what your life will look like ten, twenty, thirty years in the future, asking you to name the things that are negatively impacting your life today that you believe you cannot change. Once again, naming the problem is solving half the problem. Once these issues are named, you are asked to visualize your life in the future if no changes are made.

1. What emotions do you feel?
2. What regrets do you have?
3. If you could do it all over again, what would you change?
4. Are you proud of the choices you made?
5. Did you accomplish the things that were most important to you?
6. Did you leave a legacy for others?

This exercise gives us the ability to see our lives in the future as we near the finish line of life. I have gone through this exercise, and it was one of the most rewarding and amazing experiences of my life. Tapping deep into our emotions, it gives us the power and energy to change today and take powerful, proactive, intentional steps in our lives to make changes and to chart a course that will help us live the lives we aspire to so we can one day be proud of the time we spent and finish well. Although a trained facilitator can help in the process, all of us can spend time in meditation and prayer, reflecting on our past, present, and future to ascertain the things we desperately need to change today so that we may live the lives we will be proud of tomorrow and into the future.

At this point in the book we have defined the problem. We know we need to Revector, Repurpose, Reinvent, or Renew our careers. We know where we are currently, having taken an assessment of our strengths and weaknesses, and we have a well-defined goal (target) of what we want and where we want to be and we are building the steps we need to get there. We are acquiring new skills and becoming lifelong learners, knowing how important that is for our future. We are now making plans to overcome common obstacles and build momentum in our daily actions to get there. We have seen the

Our discipline equals our freedom.

results of those who diet for a few days and then take a break, going back to old habits, only to get upset and start the diet again a week or so later. They may lose weight, but they'll also feel guilty and frustrated. For us to gain momentum and accomplish this career change, we must take action toward our desired goal. We have to be "All in, all the time." Joko Willnik, Navy SEAL commander of the most decorated military unit in the Iraq war, is famed for saying, "Discipline equals freedom!"[2] In our context, during a time when we are planning on making a transition, this is especially true. Our discipline equals our freedom. We must be relentlessly focused on our goal, with total discipline every day in pursuing the tasks we need to do to achieve that goal. Making a pivot is a full-time job. There are no breaks, no off days, no stopping.

"ENTHUSIASM IS COMMON, ENDURANCE IS RARE."—Angela Duckworth

My Marine Corps Marathon experience opened my eyes. I learned a lot that I have applied not only to the realm of athletics but to business and other areas of my life. Many people have the enthusiasm and passion to start something difficult or challenging, but fewer have the endurance to see it through. Anything worthwhile achieving will be difficult, and when things are difficult only those with the endurance to persevere to the end will achieve success. Making a career transition will not be easy. I have found that those who have success in this area focus on three things.

1. Total focus on the goal—for as long as it takes.
2. Taking consistent daily action—no breaks.
3. Listen to your coach—leverage a support group and enlist your network!

All three are necessary for success. One without the other leads to similar results as my Marine Corps Marathon. My "result" in that race was sitting shivering in a dirty ditch, wrapped in a woman's filthy fleece, while munching on a discarded, half-eaten PowerBar, waiting helplessly for someone to take me back to the medical tent. That is a result, an outcome that I don't ever want to repeat in any area of my life. It's humbling and somewhat funny now to talk about, but at the time it was painful and embarrassing, and I lost an opportunity to do something really cool that day. I'll never get that opportunity again. There is no do-over for that day, that race . . . it is forever gone. I was, of course, able to learn from that mistake and have other opportunities in the future, but it is important to note that in life we are not guaranteed second chances and we need to make the most of the opportunities we are given. Just like my race, there are no do-overs in life. We need to make it count.

> **I lost an opportunity to do something really cool that day.**

A critical point I learned from that race is that I could not do it on my own. Actually, when I tried, I made a mess of it. It is important to get outside help and enlist the help of your network of friends and contacts when you are in the process of making a career change. This has to be done the right way. If you are unemployed and looking for a job, the entire world needs to know. Everyone! It may sound strange, but many people can be a bit coy with this information. I have worked with countless people who position themselves as "consultants," offering to help on a project or part-time basis. I am left thinking they left their previous company to start a consulting practice, which many people do and are very successful with it in this new freelance economy. However, if your true aim is to get hired quickly by a company, presenting yourself as a consultant is not the way to do it. Your network will never be able to help you. Many times after sitting down with people like this, it will come out that they are actually looking for full-time work, at which point things totally change. I now know their specific need and desire, and I can keep my eyes and ears open for opportunities and try to help them in their search.

A prominent vice president of the Robert Half Placement Service Organization in New York says that most opportunities are being found through a personal network of contacts and references, and recommendations from someone are an effective way to open doors. With many positions not publicly advertised, you will never learn of the available options unless you let people know that you are available and looking for your next opportunity. Multiple industry sources say anywhere from 70 to 80 percent of the current job openings are not advertised publicly or on job websites. To tap into this market you need to let your network know you are available.[3]

As a side note, since 2010 "consultant" in many circles has become a code word for unemployed. There are those who are full-time consultants but most who advertise themselves as consultants on LinkedIn and other job sites are seen by industry insiders as unemployed. If you are looking for a full-time job, don't do it by pretending to be a consultant!

You must also be very specific. This goes back to our goal that we are focused on. The more specific we are, the better. "I am open for new opportunities" is too general, and people will have no idea how to help. I've had friends that say, "I don't want to limit my options. I'll do anything. I just want to leave this company. Anything is better than this." That may be the way they feel, but it can't be the way you market yourself. The more specific you are, the more your network will be able to help you. What is most important to you, career advancement or quality of life? You need to know and rank an order-specific list accordingly. Knowing what you want is very important. If you can't clearly write this down, you don't have a plan. For example, if career advancement was top priority, your list might look like this.

Career-Focused Pivot Specifics

1. I want to work with X company or in X industry.
2. I want to work on X project or get experience on X team.
3. I am looking for X position or title.
4. I am looking for X development opportunities/responsibilities.
5. My anticipated pay range is $X to $X.
6. I am looking to work with X leader or have the opportunity to be mentored by X.

These are all very focused on moving up the corporate ladder, gaining experience, and positioning yourself for future promotions and opportunities. Secondary to this would be quality of life issues such as the following:

Quality of Life Pivot Specifics

1. I want to live in X city, state, or region of the country.
2. I want to live in the country, city, near the beach, in the mountains, etc.
3. I want my commute to be less than X.
4. I want to work in a laid-back, low-stress family environment.
5. I want the ability to work nine to five without overtime or travel requirements.
6. I want X benefit package.

These specifics are more about quality of life. Depending on where you are in your career and your goals, your list will be composed of similar "wants" but will need to be rank-ordered from most to least important. Generally, you will have to make some concessions. It is rare that you find the perfect unicorn that fills all your requirements. My wife and I joke because her desired requirements are all based on quality of life, and her dream location is to have property in the mountains near the beach. We joke about the limited places on earth where this is a possibility. You will need to know what you are willing to sacrifice, what you are willing to compromise on, to achieve your current goals for the stage of life you are in.

You want your network engaged, but they all can't be your coach. This is a role for a different person to play. Just as an athlete, regardless of their proficiency in a sport, needs a coach, so does everyone when making a transition like this. Tom Brady, Stephen Curry, Serena Williams, and Lindsey Vonn may all dominate their sports, but they still need a coach to show them their blind spots, encourage them past obstacles and defeats, and develop them for the challenges that lie ahead. Even the top business leaders guiding the largest and most respected global companies all have personal coaches helping them with their blind spots and to improve as leaders and executives. This is a resource many people do not seek out but should. During a transition it is needed more than ever! Finding a mentor or coach who can help you is easier than you might think. You might have two or three key people whom you ask to help you make your pivot. Each of them should have a different skill set. Here is how to get started and whom to look for.

SPONSOR/MENTOR/ADVISOR
—FAST-FORWARD WITH THEIR HELP

You need someone who has specific knowledge of the industry you are pivoting into, someone with enough business acumen to be able to help you in the process. Having a sounding board to bounce ideas off, someone who can tell you of your blind spots, is critical during this time. Although a good coach or mentor is generally someone who has walked the path ahead of you and can provide insight on what you are about to experience, they can't be so far ahead that their experience is no longer relevant. Everyone can teach us something, but having mentors tell you about their pivot experience in the 1970s is going to be less relevant than someone who just did it a few years ago. As much as possible you need timeless wisdom and principles, but applied to a modern context with current realities. I have found the three most important qualities of a mentor/sponsor are industry-specific knowledge, network, and a true desire to help you.

Everyone needs to know how to leverage LinkedIn. Programmers need to know how to use Github.com, while other professionals will need to be able to leverage Pathbrite.com. Each pivot is different and requires special attention based on the desired outcome. Many people will hire agencies to help them with their résumés, online and in-person interviewing preparation, personality assessments, and many other details. I highly recommend using these services. Your pivot will be setting you up for the next step in your career. It could be a few years, a decade, or more with hundreds of thousands of dollars on the line. People spend tens of thousands on a college degree to help them transition into the career world. Spending a few hundred dollars to get experts to prepare you for your next career is some of the best money you can invest in yourself. Don't do this alone!

I recommend that those seeking to pivot find someone who can help them with the *business and operational side* of the transition. Try to find someone who is knowledgeable, networked, has industry experience, and can help in a wide variety of ways. You are not looking for them to do the work; that is all on you. You are asking them for advice and perspective, and if possible to open doors and maybe make a connection or two if they know of a job opening. The people most likely to help you in this capacity are friends and associates in your current network. I don't recommend calling some local CEO asking for this type of help, especially if you don't have a relationship with them.

The second person you will need to get some advice from is someone who will help you with the *emotional roller coaster* that you will be on. You are never more lost than during a transition when everything in your life has been turned upside down. Many times your identity is lost. Men in our culture especially have a hard time with this as our identity so often is tied to our jobs, our titles, the ability to provide for our families. If you are in a forced transition (lost a job, fired, laid off), this is extremely painful. I have seen depression set in, along with the fear of finding the next job. Many are consumed with self-doubt. Having a support network that understands what you are going through and can help you is important. There will be highs and lows, with exciting opportunities

God wants us reliant on Him and seeking His guidance.

and potential disappointments along the way if an offer you were counting on falls through. Discouragement is something everyone faces, and just like a coach helps an athlete after a defeat to get prepared for the next competition, you will need that person in your life. Having your pastor, small group, and other friends pray for and with you during this time is important.

Personally, it is during these seasons of my life where my personal faith grew the most. Just as my coach reminded me years earlier that we learn more from our mistakes than our victories, I have found that it is during seasons of challenge and difficulty where our character and integrity is tested and formed. Our faith grows strong because we realize that although we must work hard and do our part, we are still reliant on God to be faithful and help us through these challenges. When things are going well, it is hard for us to see God's hand of providence working in our lives. We can be distracted and think that any success we have is due to our own hard work and efforts. I know I have fallen into that trap at times. God wants us reliant on Him and seeking His guidance. He has been there during my darkest hours when I was alone and I thought there was nothing more that I could do—then I saw God miraculously work through others to answer my prayers and open doors. He will do the same for you. Your prayer partners are the greatest assets you have on this journey! More important than pivoting into the job of your dreams and into the next chapter of your life is seeing and experiencing God in a real and visceral way that many times we are not able to experience when our lives are running perfectly on autopilot.

> **➤ PIVOT POINTS** What is your why? Is it big enough?

Author Simon Sinek has become famous for his "Start with Why" TED Talk video, which has been viewed over 27 million times.[4] If you have not seen this, I encourage you to take eighteen minutes to view the content. It is absolutely worth it. Simon argues that more important than WHAT we do, and HOW we do it, is WHY we do it. He encourages people to always start with why, and I am encouraging you to do the same here.

We know that to make changes in our life we will have to overcome continued fear and doubt, which will be daily obstacles in our way. We will need to overcome a fear of failure and loss aversion. It is easy to design plans and dream about the future, but it is much more difficult to be disciplined each day to take massive action, which builds momentum toward our goal. We must be relentlessly focused on our goal, take daily actions toward it, and have coaches/mentors who will be able to help us along the way. One coach needs to be able to offer practical help, while another coach or group of people needs to be a support network to encourage and motivate us on the journey. Because of the obstacles you will face, you need to have a very big why. What is motivating you to make this change? What are your goals? In this chapter we spoke about the "Dickens Process," looking into the future to see your life and analyzing the emotions you feel about what you see. Are you on the right track to achieve your goals? Are you happy with what you see? If not, what do you need to do to change that outcome? You are in control, and decisions and actions you take today will impact your future. So here are the action steps for this chapter.

1. *Dickens Process*—Go through this with a friend or family. Get real, go deep, and be honest with yourself. Write down what you learn through this process. It will be powerful in helping motivate you to change.

2. *Placement Firms*—When making a pivot to a new career, it is critical to enlist all the resources at your disposal. Let your entire network know what you are trying to do, and start building relationships with local and national

placement firms. You want your résumé in their files. Here are a few of the firms I know that have great reputations.

- Robert Half Placement Services
- Korn Ferry
- VACO
- Diag Partners

Make sure to look for smaller local firms that are operating in your hometown or the place where you are looking to relocate. Many times local firms are leveraged by local businesses to fill their open positions. You can also search for recruiters and placement services using LinkedIn and also RileyGuide.com.

3. **Get Specific**—Don't contact a recruiter or placement firm until you have spent a lot of time really understanding what you are looking for. Review the pivot specifics of this chapter and zero in on your specifics. The more specific you are, the greater your opportunity for success.

4. **Your Résumé**—Start developing your résumé. If you already have one, update it with all the current information. If you don't have one, start collecting data as far back as possible and putting it into an official document. This should not be longer than two pages. For an example of a professional résumé, go to my website, www.RobertDickie.com, and under the Downloads tab you can download a *Life Plan: Success Guide* that I have used for many people to help them get started.

CURRENTS OF GROWTH AND OPPORTUNITY

"Should you find yourself in a chronically leaking boat, energy devoted to changing vessels is likely to be more productive than energy devoted to patching leaks."

WARREN BUFFETT

Warren Buffett, the "Oracle of Omaha," considered the most successful investor in the world, has had an amazing tenure building Berkshire Hathaway by investing in companies and industries over the past sixty years. Known for investing in undervalued companies and growing them to new heights or getting into up-and-coming industries before they had long periods of record growth, Mr. Buffett knows how to spot a winner and invest in it at the right time. When you are making your career pivot, you need to make a similar bet and look for the same results. You don't want to be the person pivoting into horse-carriage production at the time Henry Ford is launching the Model T. You would be making a successful transition into a career field that is dying and going out of business. Where are the currents of growth and opportunity in the new economy that will take you along with them?

Advice that Warren Buffett gave a young man at one of his companies is very applicable to those making a pivot today. Buffett was visiting one of the companies that he and Berkshire Hathaway had invested in. The company executives had gathered and were providing reports on the various operations, divisions, and product lines of this company. One young manager got up to give a report and was talking about the difficulty of meeting sales targets for a particular product line. Quarter after quarter, the margins were thin, and a lot of work was going into trying to revitalize this product line so it could be successful in the marketplace. After studying the numbers and hearing the reports, Buffett asked the young executive why he was working so hard fighting the current for such a small margin. Why not find a strong current in the marketplace where the customers are heading and come up with a product line or service that places you and your business in the middle of that fast-moving stream?

It was a paradigm shift for the team. We know we need to work hard, but we also need to work smart!

If you have ever done open-water swimming in the ocean, you know how powerful currents can be. I lived in Hawaii for three years and loved spending weekends kayaking and surfing on the North Shore of Oahu. When the surf was up, fighting the currents was almost impossible. As a surfer, you were taught that if you got caught in a current taking you out to sea, you should not fight it but go with it, saving your energy, and start to swim parallel to the beach until you were able to work your way out of the current and then swim back to shore. Warren Buffett understood this principle, applied to business as well as currents and trends, that we can waste our time and energy fighting when we should be looking for ways to leverage them for our benefit. As you make a pivot in your career, you must realize that it will take a lot of hard work, dedication, and commitment to your goal. Make sure that time and energy spent pivoting to a new career is going to be worth it and net good results for you for the future. You want to put yourself in these positive currents that will provide you opportunity while avoiding bad currents (industries/companies) that are in a downward spiral.

The two most painful company currents to be in look like this:

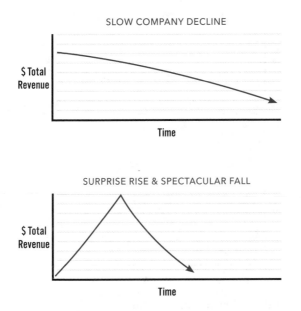

SLOW COMPANY DECLINE

SURPRISE RISE & SPECTACULAR FALL

You might find yourself with an opportunity to join an organization or industry that is in a downward trend. Early in my career I was a hired-gun turnaround specialist, I know how difficult these situations can be. Even if you are not being hired to turn around a company or organization, you will be along for the ride and you will be putting your faith and future in the hands of the management and leadership team, hoping they will be able to do their part to right the ship. Trying to reverse long trend lines is very difficult and not generally in your favor. I know this from firsthand experience, having worked with multiple companies in different industries that found themselves in this position. All things being equal, wouldn't you like to place yourself in a fast current where the same effort you expend nets you greater results? That is what we are looking for, and in today's economy those currents exist. You are looking for an industry or company current whose trend line looks like this:

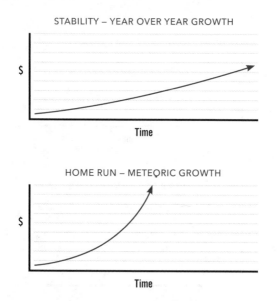

STABILITY – YEAR OVER YEAR GROWTH

$

Time

HOME RUN – METEORIC GROWTH

$

Time

Proper due diligence on the front end will allow you to know where there are great opportunities and industry growth where you can spend the next chapter of your career growing, developing, learning new skills, having an impact, and enjoying an exciting ride. No matter what, you are going to have to work hard. Why not work hard and work smart, putting yourself in the best place for future growth and career success? Eric Weinstein, managing partner at Thiel Capital, says, "It's better to be in an expanding world and not exactly in the right field than to be in a contracting world where people's worst behavior comes out."[1]

This is one of the most powerful statements I have heard, because it rings so true to me. I have witnessed it firsthand and I am sure you have as well. Although it is important to find fulfillment and enjoyment in what we do, I have seen people who had the perfect job for their career goals but were miserable because they were in an industry that was dying, or with a company that was losing market share to competitors and had no chance to make up ground. When in these environments, stress is everywhere. People backstab and compete for limited resources for their pet projects, forgetting the overall mission of

Everyone wants to be on a winning team.

the organization. A scarcity mentality takes over and people are constantly fearful for their jobs and wondering if the doors will close next month or next year. It really brings out the worst in many people. The opposite is also true in an environment with good leadership, growth plans, and companies that have the ability to focus and are in sectors of growth and prosperity. Teams come together, create exciting new plans, execute with perfection, and although there is stress to achieve, it is a different kind of stress and an environment that people long for. Everyone wants to be on a winning team.

This is the type of environment we need to be creating at our work or searching for. These are the types of environments that will bring out your best and you will have the highest potential to succeed. So where are some of these potential growth sectors for the future where these positive currents might carry us to success, and what can we do to add the skills needed to transition into those sectors?

Tim Ferriss, the *New York Times* bestselling author of *The Four-Hour Work Week* and host of *The Tim Ferriss Show*, has interviewed people like Arnold Schwarzenegger, Jamie Foxx, BJ Novak, Kevin Costner, Peter Thiel, Seth Rogan, Kevin Rose, and Ed Catmull, to list a few. His guests include movie stars, business icons, athletes, executives, authors, and many more. The one thing they all have in common is they have achieved great success in their field of endeavor and Tim wants to know why and how. A favorite question he asks of many of them is—if they had to start all over again at the age of eighteen with $1,000 to their name, what would they do? This is a great exercise for us to consider, and for me the answer is simple. I would get a job or start a business and stay debt-free using that $1,000 to follow Laurie Pickard's formula at NoPayMBA.com to get an MBA equivalent by taking courses at the top business schools in the world, paying only for the certifications to show that I passed the classes. I would also look for jobs where I could grow sales experience as that is an increasingly important skill in this new economy. I would continue to use those skills to leverage up into better jobs with more opportunity in one of the following career fields. I could add to this list for now, after all my research and interviewing, these are the sectors I am personally very excited about. If you're looking for the positive-growth trend lines mentioned above, these are the industries and skill sets that will offer massive opportunity over the next decade. If you are looking for a career transition into a field with great potential, the following are just a few areas you should investigate.

Green and Renewable Energy

The promise of green and renewable energy has been something that scientists and environmentalists have sought after like the Holy Grail for years. Until now, what has held back the growth of this sector is technology that did not allow it to affordably scale to the masses without huge governmental subsidies. That is changing. With technological improvements and drastic cost reductions, these energy sources are now quickly becoming affordable and will help revolutionize the world. Frankly, Europe is far ahead of the United States in this area. This is creating a current that is gaining momentum, has global government backing and interest, and is supported by popular demand. The poster child for this movement at the moment is Elon Musk and Tesla Motors and Solar City. His Tesla cars to this point have been works of art and performance, but mostly outside the price range of the average driver, with the Model S and X costing from $57,000 to $105,000 with a limited range of 240 to 250 miles. However, in 2016, the new Model III will be released with a price tag around $30,000, a range of three-hundred-plus miles, and the performance of a BMW.[2] This will revolutionize the auto industry, and it is just the beginning. To learn more about how Musk is revolutionizing multiple industries, I highly recommend reading the biography *Elon Musk* by Ashlee Vance, and then watching Elon's launch of the Model X at www.RobertDickie.com. Tesla is pioneering functions like "autopilot," which allows the car to be driven autonomously on the highway while you sit back in your seat and sleep or read on your way to work. Astro Teller, leading Google X, is also working on a driverless car project as the rush to deliver this to the market is underway. The widespread assumption is that driverless cars will be on the roads in less than three years and that

Homes very soon will be able to go "off the grid" and be totally energy-independent.

most children under the age of five today will never drive a car.

Tesla is also leading the charge in ion-battery development, and each Tesla car will come with a battery-charging unit installed in homes for the vehicles to be recharged at night. Combine this with the revolution in solar panels that can power an entire home and store unused energy in home batteries, and then sell the unused energy to the electrical companies, and we have another revolution underway.

The price of solar panels continues to drop, while their effectiveness is increasing. Companies around the country are popping up to install solar panels on homes, and those with battery packs, like the Tesla, not only can power their homes and vehicles but are able to store the excess power generated and sell it back to the energy companies. In effect, homes very soon will be able to go "off the grid" and be totally energy independent.

The impact of this new revolution on the power and auto industries is certain, but the effects will not be known for a while. What we do know is that the ion battery and solar industries will continue to grow exponentially. Home building will change, and suppliers to retrofit old homes with these devices will rapidly grow. Whole industries are currently sprouting up to figure out how to build charging stations for electric vehicles around the country. How do we create the infrastructure for electric vehicles as we have for gas vehicles? It will happen fast. Remember when phone booths and pay phones were everywhere in the malls, hotels, schools, airports? Now they are gone . . . vanished. Industries can change overnight, and the green/renewable energy revolution will have the same impact on our economy. When the cellphone revolution took place, those who were in the business of making and installing phone booths got hurt. Don't be in today's version of a pay-phone business—look at how you can connect to the new energy boom. You don't have to be selling cars for Tesla, building Trina solar panels, or engineering new ion batteries with LG. There are thousands of companies and opportunities that will be connected on the periphery of this revolution, helping it grow and expand. Whether you are in engineering, programming, social media, marketing, teaching, or many other fields, the question to ask is, "If this coming revolution is something I am excited about and believe in, how do I take my current skill sets and abilities and engage and get connected to this sector?" It is up to you to connect those dots by adding skills and finding out how you can add value to the companies that are leading this charge. You don't have to be an engineer, scientist, or technologist to work at one of these companies. If you feel you are in a "pay phone" business today, figure out a way to transition to a company in a growth market. These companies need people in all the basic business functions—HR, accounting, marketing, sales, and more.

Start planning your pivot to an industry with upside potential while you can. It can be done and if you decide to latch on for the ride it will be a wild and exciting one for sure! Have you ever wondered what it would be like to have experienced the railroad or automobile revolutions in the nineteenth and twentieth centuries? This will be the modern-day equivalent.

Technology

Silicon Valley venture capitalist Marc Andreessen famously said that "software is eating the world," and we have already highlighted aspects of that revolution in this book. Every industry, market segment, and business is being impacted by new technologies that transform back-office operations, engagement with customers, product development, and marketing. Even support functions from human resources (HR), legal, and accounting are undergoing automation and technological shifts in the way they support and bring value to businesses. I am continually asked by college students what they should study and what fields they should pursue. I firmly believe in using assessments to make sure you are in alignment with your passions and giftings, but once that is done you have a choice. Given the choice between two careers that are aligned with your skills and passions, always "tech up"! Doing what you love in a dying industry or in a job and career that cannot provide for your needs is no fun. Anything remotely related to technology is in high demand. Those choosing courses of study should consider that majors in STEM fields (Science, Technology, Engineering, and

Math) are in high demand. An administrator at a prominent East Coast university told me the average starting salary for those in nontechnical career fields for their graduates was around $35,000 a year, while those with STEM degrees started around $75,000 to $80,000 per year.

When people think of careers in technology, the areas of coding and programming come to mind, but these are not the only fields to consider. A senior executive of the Robert Half Placement in New York says, "So many people see the tech boom happening right now and think, 'I am not a techie. I can't take advantage of this,' and that is just wrong! Tech is creating all sorts of new jobs in content creation and creative environments. Companies need photographers and writers for website content. Companies need people to help with user engagements. They are hiring SEO (Search Engine Optimization) strategists that understand social media. You don't have to be a programmer to excel in the tech environment!" Salary guides like Salary.com show that in 2015 salaries grew by 4 percent but by more than 5 percent in the tech sector. The tech sector also has the lowest unemployment rate and the greatest anticipated growth potential over the next twenty years.

> **Global development is entering a new era where technology allows us to make rapid improvements in the lives of the world's poor.**

Furthermore, Reggie Leonard, career advisor for the University of Virginia, says he hears students all the time say, "I want to be in a tech company." He replies, "Are you kidding? Every company today is a tech company. There is no company out in the marketplace where technology isn't the backbone of the operation or having an impact on it. Tech is everywhere!"

So what are some of the big advancements and trends in tech?

You will start to hear more about "computer vision" or "visual search" in the coming months. This technology allows a user to use their smartphone camera to hover over an object and highlight it and immediately search the Internet for that object. This ties into data science that we will talk about shortly, but this will revolutionize the way we search and shop. Those concerned about environmental sustainability, and that should be everyone who is breathing, will notice quantum leaps in how technology allows us to become more sustainable and green in the way we build cities and support our populations. Global development is also entering a new era where technology and sensors allow us to make rapid improvements in the lives of the world's poor and in emerging countries. Just one example: placing sensors on wells in Africa enables health officials to track the spread of contagions and disease faster than ever, allowing for quicker deployment of vaccines when outbreaks occur. Once again, the reams of data that are being produced with all the sensors are creating new opportunities for data scientists who monitor this.

Education Technology, or "EdTech," is currently undergoing a massive revolution and will continue to for some time. Mark Zuckerberg, founder of Facebook, has committed a large portion of his personal fortune to the advancement of EdTech. MOOCs (Massive Open Online Courses) that many universities are loading online are democratizing education, but this is just the first wave of change. Trailblazers are looking for the "gamification" of education to make it as enjoyable and addictive for children as their video games. Ever see a young child play a video game for hours trying to beat levels, win contests, defeat villains, and win badges? Well, education is moving in that direction as well. Would you like to be a part of that? Or how about the emergence of telemedicine? This is not telemedicine for you and me. It is telemedicine and training for doctors and nurses. With the advancement of medicine and technology over the past decade, those who graduated from medical school or nursing school in 2005 might as well have graduated decades ago. Things have changed that much in just a decade. Telemedicine will allow doctors and nurses to receive training online to keep up with the latest advancements and procedures. ArcheMedX is a company to watch for in this space, at the forefront of these new technologies.

For those who want to read up on technology advancements and have a better understanding of new disruptive technologies coming our way, here are a few of my favorite places to do research and stay current on tech topics.

TECH CRUNCH—Website for all major tech news.

WILDCARD—Download this app and set your filter to get all the latest tech news.

10 THOUGHTS BY JACK MARA—Follow this blog (10thoughts .com)—Jack is fantastic!

PRODUCT HUNT—Explore the new inventions and ideas that are getting funded on this website. These are leading innovators.

QUORA.COM—If you have a question on anything tech, you can submit it here and get some fantastic answers and insight.

Block Chain Technology (Bitcoin)

Bitcoin, the crypto-currency that was invented by Satoshi Nakamoto in 2008 and unleashed on the world in 2009, is the world's first truly digital currency.[3] Bitcoin is now growing globally as a payment method because, unlike a US dollar, Euro, Chinese Yuan or any other currency that is backed by a government, this currency is not state-sponsored. It is open source and not controlled by politicians and bankers, making it safer in the eyes of many who have witnessed the profligate spending of global governments.

The real revolution is the back-end technology called block chain, which is a permission-less distributed database. Digital strategist Don Tapscott says it is the greatest invention since the World Wide Web and describes block chain as "a global spreadsheet . . . where information can be stored in a way that is immutable, incorruptible, and unchangeable."[4] Many have heard of Bitcoin but are far less informed about the new technology that makes this possible. The ramifications are already rippling around the globe as industries look to leverage "the greatest new technology of a generation."

Barclays Bank became the first bank to accept Bitcoin as a form of payment, with many more like Commonwealth Bank of Australia, Credit Suisse, and J.P. Morgan Chase following suit. With few people in the loop regarding this technology, those who have basic understanding of it and its principles are in high demand. To learn more about Bitcoin and what it can do, search for the Bitcoin video on KhanAcademy.org. How is this expanding to impact our lives tomorrow? If we can remove paper currency from our system in a trusted manner with block chain technology, what else can we remove? People are now testing this technology for voting, which could be done on our cellphones and handheld devices. Block chain technology will be used to change many things in our life, from online banking to voting. For those who feel like they missed out on the initial wave of the dot-com boom, this is the next wave starting to build.

"Internet of Things"

We are entering an age where everything that can will have a microprocessor in it that will connect that device to the Internet, relaying important information to our devices. For example, people can now use their phone to open and close garage doors and other doors, monitor video cameras in their homes, adjust their thermostats, and even receive notification of smoke detector alarms going off.

You can put a device in your Nike running shoes to track your steps and pace, while your watch will monitor your heart rate, uploading this to a digital health account. Under Armour is setting the standard with Bluetooth-enabled shoes that connect to their wristbands and heart rate monitor. They have also partnered up with IBM Watson to sync your personal data with data from similar users like you for comparative analysis. You can monitor your fitness within your demographic and see where you should be average regarding health and fitness. Record App asks you, "How do you feel?" on a rating scale. They plan to aggregate that data over time to help predict, based on your workout or behavior earlier in the day, how you will feel, based on your current activity and what you can do to feel better. Imagine getting a text message warning you, "Based on your activity over the past few hours you will feel like a 3 at 5:00 p.m. today. To feel like a 9 out of 10 as you leave work you should . . ."

This is coming! You can even order a special Internet-connected cup that will track the ounces of water you consume each day. When you run out of laundry detergent, you can press an Amazon Dash button in your laundry room and an order will instantly be sent to your home. For aspiring inventors and entrepreneurs, the advice I most often hear given in classrooms and "shark tank" environments is to think of a commonly used daily item that does not have a microchip in it—and make one. Everything that we use will at some point have a microchip and be connected to the Internet. Ralph Lauren has launched a line of workout clothing with chips in it connecting it to the Internet, allowing it to monitor your heart rate, energy exertion, and steps taken. The company is currently working on a polo shirt that will do the same thing. Astro Teller and his team at Google X continue to work on ventures like Project Loon, whose goal is to deliver free Wi-Fi to every inch of the globe by creating a network of balloons flying in the stratosphere with wireless routers that will beam Wi-Fi to every person on the planet.[5] The Internet of things will continue to explode. How can you position yourself to be a part of this revolution? What companies are leading this charge? What industries are ripe for disruption because of connected devices? What devices and services will consumers want? Finally, where will all this data that is collected go and who will analyze it? That brings us to the next hot spot!

Big Data

We are in the midst of a data explosion. IBM reports that 90 percent of the world's total collected and usable information from the beginning of recorded time to today has been collected in the last two years.[6] Think about that! The world now produces 2.5 quintillion bytes of data a day! In 2012, Harvard Business School said the "sexiest" job of the century would be a data scientist.[7] Uh—Houston, we have a problem. At that moment there were no college programs teaching, training, or growing data scientists. You literally could not get a degree in this field. It was a field created almost overnight, underlining the claim that 65 percent of the jobs of the future don't even exist today.[8]

Let that sink in for a moment. Think things are changing fast? We are training our children for jobs that don't even exist; worst yet, the education system was designed for a bygone era and jobs that no longer exist. (We can save that topic for another time.)

Overnight a few leading universities quickly jumped into action to create degree programs for data scientists. The University of Virginia was at the leading edge and within two years launched their data scientist degree program. Each year more schools launch data science degree programs, so chances are there is one near you. As of this year UVA will have graduated over ninety candidates. Reggie Leonard, Career Services Director for the Data Science Institute at

UVA, says demand is incredible. "Our students are being recruited in the middle of the program with multiple and competitive job offers. They have their pick of what company they want to work with." With starting salaries at $80,000 and above, these graduates will work in all major industries, as every company today needs a data scientist.

But what do data scientists actually do? Leonard notes, "People need to understand this discipline is broken down into very different components. Data science is predictive. Data Analytics is more retroactive (reporting) which is what has been done in the past. Analytics are very important and will continue to grow in demand, but it tends to stop at the point of looking at data that has been collected in order to understand things that happened in the past. The new, growing area is Data Science, where we can take data in real time and use it to predict outcomes, and forecast changes that allow us to run business more efficiently. We are at a point where we can literally teach machines how to learn, based on data that we feed them. Further, we are at a point where we know how to encode nearly everything as data."

If you are wondering what to do for your career and want to place yourself in the midst of a fast-moving current where you will be in major demand for decades to come, explore the options around a degree or skill sets in data science. If you would like to learn more, check out Coursera.org. They have two Nanodegrees that I would recommend: Introduction to Data Science by Washington University and Data Science by Johns Hopkins University. Furthermore, before this went to print, Microsoft just launched its own Nanodegree in data science. (You can learn more at Microsoft.)

A business associate of mine was just at the Google head-quarters in California, speaking with people, and the topic of data scientists came up. They said they could not get enough of these experts and that they were hiring people who had completed the data science

Nanodegrees from these institutions. Think about that for a moment. This is an online microdegree that you can earn from home, averaging about ten to fifteen hours of work per week, taking about six to nine months to complete. The total cost: about $470! Google is watching the program and the people who are graduating with top scores and they are calling them for interviews, asking them to join their team!

Regardless of what industry you are in, changes are coming that will revolutionize it.

If you are looking for a career pivot, you don't have to spend four years and $100,000 to get a new degree. Get a Nanodegree in a growing market segment where there is a fast-rushing current, and get pulled along with the trend. It takes some time and effort, but those willing to make the pivot can do it and transition into some of the top companies in the world.

These five areas are just a few explosive growth segments in the global economy over the next few decades that you could consider as "pivot-worthy." Regardless of what industry you are in, changes are coming that will revolutionize it. The key is to be on the front end of that change as one implementing change and making things better. You don't want to be the one fighting change or the one with your head in the sand, hoping you will not be impacted by what is going on around you. For those looking for greater opportunity and growth, we need to be looking for a bigger bowl.

NON-TECH OPPORTUNITIES

You might be wondering, "Bob, are there any opportunities for non-tech people? How about us hardworking liberal arts folks?" The news has been filled with the success of the whiz kids, teenage tech founders who became billionaires, MBAs, and engineers. The pendulum is shifting, and new opportunities are developing for those with a different skill set. Daniel Pink outlines the shift taking place in his book *A Whole New Mind*, saying, "The era of left-brain dominance, and the Information Age that it engendered, are giving way to a new world in which the right brain qualities of inventiveness, meaning, empathy will predominate."[9] He goes on to say, "We are moving from an economy and society built on the logical, linear, computer-like capabilities of the Information Age to an economy and society built on the inventive, empathic, big-picture capabilities of what's rising in its place, the Conceptual Age."

As jobs and industries continue to move to low-wage markets around the globe, and automation impacts entry-level jobs from fast-food restaurants to accounting firms, Daniel Pink artfully explains the skills of "High Concept" and "High Touch" that are becoming very valuable in our new economy, since they can't be off-shored or automated away. "High concept involves the capacity to detect patterns and opportunities, to create artistic and emotional beauty, to craft a satisfying narrative, and to combine seemingly unrelated ideas into something new. High touch involves that ability to empathize with others, to understand the subtleties of human interaction, to find joy in one's self and to elicit it in others, and to stretch to purpose and meaning."[10] If you are a "right-brained" person who has felt left behind, wondering if there is opportunity for you, this is a book I strongly encourage you to read.

THE GOLDFISH PRINCIPLE

At this point you might find yourself asking, "Should I stay or should I go?" All these new opportunities for growth and development seem exciting. For those who have lost a job, I hope you are encouraged to see that transition as a door closing in your past to allow you to craft a plan to jump on board a new opportunity that could have vastly more potential in your future. For those considering a change or those who are in the midst of the process, I think it is important to remember the "Goldfish Principle."

Those who have children and have had the pleasure (using my sarcastic voice) of having a goldfish as a family pet might be aware of this principle. Oddly, a goldfish will only grow as big as their bowl allows them to. You can take two identical goldfish from the same family and put one in a small bowl and one in a very large bowl, and in a short time you will see a shocking difference. Their growth rates will be identical; and then the fish in the smaller bowl will eventually stop growing while the fish in the bigger bowl will continue to grow. This strange governor on growth for fish can also be observed in our own lives. You can take two people with similar academic backgrounds and skill sets and place them in two different environments and they will progress differently, based on the environment they are in. Proverbs 27:17 says, "As iron sharpens iron, so one person sharpens another." Believe it or not, our environment, peers, manager, and boss will have a huge impact on our growth and careers. Everyone should be striving to be a lifelong learner, but there is only so much you can do on your own. The "bowl" (your job and its environment) that you place yourself in will determine a lot about your growth and potential in the years ahead. You will grow to the potential of your organization, your peers, the leadership of the company, and the totality of the environment you are in.

I have seen this time and time again with people who took different career paths early in life and years later they are worlds apart from their peers, based on the environments they placed themselves in. Don't settle! If you find yourself in an environment and you are questioning the organization's commitment to excellence, the leadership's ability to execute, or you just are not getting challenged to grow with new opportunities, the only way for you to grow is to find a new, bigger bowl. The longer you stay in a stagnant environment,

The longer you stay in a stagnant environment, the more damage you will do to your career.

the more damage you will do to your career. The people you work for are always important, but this is especially true when you are first starting out. Who you work for is more important than what you do. Will they help you and mentor you? Do they look to help you and your career advancement? Are you learning from them? Will they leverage their networks and help you, even if your goal might be to transition outside the company someday? Good bosses can help make careers, and anyone who has achieved success in the business world will tell you that along the way they had a great teacher, mentor, and boss that helped propel them forward. Be mindful of those who might be jealous of your success and try to push you down and hold you back. They are not always easy to spot, but you will feel the tension in the relationship as your career star starts to rise. Unfortunately, these insecure types are everywhere, and it is best to pivot your way out of their sphere of influence as quickly as possible.

So when you are looking for a bigger bowl to have greater challenges, development, and learning opportunities, what are things in the bowl that you should highly value? In this analysis we are not looking at making a pivot for an increase in pay. In fact, I have known people who made a career change and took a pay cut because they wanted to work for a specific company or manager where they knew they would be getting great experience and building their résumé. This is the classic "take one step backward and two steps forward." If you can pivot to a great industry-leading company or a great boss/manager that will invest in your life and help you develop, that is a great career move.

I think that all our decisions should begin with the end in mind. We have the ability to make decisions early in our career that will help us over the long term. These are a few things that we should be mindful of when making career decisions. First, the best way to get recruited in today's market is to *work for a great brand* (think Google, Nike, BMW, Amazon, General Electric, Goldman Sachs, Tesla, Ralph Lauren, Walmart, etc.). These are great, ubiquitous brands, known by everyone. When working for a big brand with great systems, there is a level of trust that companies will have with your training and experience. Most importantly, make sure the values of the company align with your personal values.

Second, *work for an industry leader.* Most of the brands I just listed would also be considered industry leaders in their sectors. Companies always want to hire away talent from industry leaders so they can bring their knowledge and expertise into the new company and help them improve and advance. The recruiting wars in Silicon Valley are legendary, as tech companies would fight for the best programmers to get inside information on their competitors.

Third, *work on an important project.* If you have been on the product development team for a highly specialized product, helped launch a new technology, or done something noteworthy in your industry, other companies will be after you to help duplicate that type of success for them. Make sure to highlight on LinkedIn.com, PathBrite.com, and other online services the accomplishments you have had. It has been said that the best predictor of a person's future achievement is what they have done in the past. Successful people leave unmistakable clues.

Fourth, *work for a great start-up or smaller operation* where you will gain tremendous experience because you will be able to work with senior leaders, serve in multiple roles within the company, and obtain industry experience many of your peers in larger operations won't have the chance to get. Many people will opt out of working at a big, brand-name company to have the chance to work in a start-up for these reasons.

Finally, *mine your network*. All business is relationships, and those with big networks of deep, multi-industry relationships that they can leverage for business are always sought after specifically for their contacts. These contacts are so valuable that many sales organizations will go after salespeople for their relationships or "book of business." In the military, many times senior officers will be recruited upon retirement by companies like Boeing, Lockheed Martin, Raytheon, and others not only for their years of experience, but also for their contacts with decision makers in the military, government, and with foreign militaries. The top professionals in your industry are no different. Remember this—all business is based on relationships. Over your career, if developed correctly, your network and relationships will become the most valuable assets you have!

When it is all said and done, to find new opportunities you have to get involved in your work, industry, and community by networking and researching. Opportunities come from taking intentional action, and your actions must align with your overall goals. Things don't magically happen on their own, and you are the only one who can take the necessary steps to get the process moving.

I am reminded of how a friend views networking. He classifies people into three groups: a giver, a taker, an exchanger. A giver is a person who, when in a relationship, is looking to provide value to others and help first and foremost. The opposite is someone who is a taker. They network and engage in relationships solely for the opportunity to take or extract value for themselves and their needs. The exchanger is a balanced position. They want to provide value but also look for that value in the relationship to be reciprocated. My friend always asks himself, "Is this person a giver, a taker, or exchanger," when he meets someone. Work hard to be a giver and then an exchanger. Takers get labeled and don't go far.

➤ PIVOT POINTS Crafting Your Story, Connecting the Dots

To make a successful pivot you have to be acutely aware of how YOU create value for others. You can't just rely on a résumé listing your job history, skills, and accolades and expect the person on the other end of the interview to be able to connect the dots. These people are busy and distracted and don't know your personal story as well as you, and might not be able to connect the dots in your career. That is your job! There are a lot of people you will be competing with, and the person who the company feels will produce the most value for them will be hired. Be ready to tell your story with data and examples. Being able to turn your résumé into a story is a powerful way to be considered for a job. You get to craft the narrative! Instead of a list of disparate experiences and skills, take the time to craft this into a single narrative framing the job you are looking at as the next logical step in your career progression. Instead of being seen as a person who is just looking for the next job to get a paycheck, be intentional in seeking out this particular job because it is in alignment with your well-thought-out career plan. Someone who is intentional and career-oriented will win out over the person who appears only to be interested in that paycheck.

Furthermore, highlight skills you have learned and how you have leveraged them for other businesses. Share success stories that could be duplicated in their operation. Show them how your skill sets and experience will bring value to their operation. This will require you to have knowledge of their business, the position you are interviewing for, their needs, and/or frustrations.

- What are industry challenges they might be having?
- Where has the industry innovated and where is it stagnant, waiting for new transformation?
- How will technology impact their industry or business?
- What problems can you help solve?
- How can you help them meet their strategic goals?

Success in life is all about helping others. The more people you are able to help, the more successful you will be. This principle is true for companies whose goal is to help as many customers as possible, from the CEO down to the entry-level employee. You have to dust off your inner salesperson and be ready to pitch and sell yourself! Connecting the dots for the person on the other end of the table on how you will help them is a winning strategy.

This should go without saying, but you should see that your narrative changes from job to job. If you are submitting a two-page résumé for a job it will be hard to put all the data points about you in two pages. You should just include the things that are most important to that job. If you are crafting a résumé for a global nonprofit one day and a manufacturing job the next, both of those documents will have a lot in common but they should also be position-specific. Building a standard résumé that you send out to everyone is a mistake. For a tool that will help you with this process, download the *Life Plan: Success Guide* at www.RobertDickie.com.

LEVERAGE FAILURE

"I have tried to learn as much as possible from prior attempts. If nothing else, we are committed to failing in a new way."
ELON MUSK

The two HMMWVs (High Mobility Multipurpose Wheeled Vehicles, or Humvees) slowly exited the All-American drop zone on Camp Robinson outside Little Rock, Arkansas, and headed up a small ridgeline bordering the 4,500-foot dirt runway. C-130 aircrews from Little Rock Air Force base, just a few miles away, used this strip to practice combat landings and perform low-altitude cargo drops from the back of the plane. On any given day, three to six planes could be seen in the distance getting lined up for a low pass over the drop zone, where crews would practice dropping fifteen-pound sandbags on the target of the drop zone. Larger drops of payloads that included 1,000-pound bundles simulating supply drops, and even 3,000-pound pallets, simulating heavy equipment drops to combat deployed troops, were conducted around the clock.

I was the flight commander of the 314th Aerial Delivery Unit, in charge of this 150-plus person team that packed the parachutes and pallets of cargo that were loaded onto the C-130s. These would then be parachuted out of the back of the plane to simulate combat resupply drops to ground troops onto the All-American and Black Jack drop zones outside of Little Rock, where air crews from all over the world came to train. We prided ourselves on the work and the daily recovery of all the loads and getting them ready for the next training cycle. My favorite times were nighttime drops, where we had to use night-vision goggles to watch the distant planes in the black sky get closer, until all you heard were the engines overhead and then saw the big canopies of the parachutes opening overhead. Operating on the drop zone was a lot of fun, and on this particular day, after the work was done, we decided to take our Humvees on a little exploring run through the two-track trails (off-road trails used by 4 x 4 vehicles) on Camp Robinson Military Installation.

As the first lieutenant in charge, I had four other new second lieutenants that had recently joined the 314th Logistics Group, and I was giving them a tour of the operation. A senior master sergeant from the group was with us taking pictures for a report he would be writing up the next day for the group commander. It wasn't long before we were testing the ruggedness of our Humvees on the unforgiving terrain. On the long stretches of open "two-track roads" we let it rip, only moments later to drive down steep embankments, through brush, and in many places carving a path where no vehicle had previously ventured. I laughed a bit as the unsuspecting passengers in the back were tossed around like an old pair of shoes in a dryer.

After we had given the new lieutenants a good tour of Camp Robinson and carved a few new trails, it was time to head back to Little Rock Air Force Base. Our adventure, however, had led us to a wide creek that needed to be traversed. The Hummer that had been following us pulled up alongside me to discuss the situation. They said they would cross first, and off they went. The flat banks of the creek had been previously flooded, creating a large mud plain. I watched the Humvee spit up a rooster tail of mud as they blazed through—and then the vehicle disappeared as a wave of water enveloped the Humvee, only to have it reappear momentarily, driving up the other side of the creek. We were greeted by a chorus of hoots and hollers as the team relished the experience and encouraged us to follow. I rolled up my window, put the vehicle in drive, and hit the gas. I got a good head of speed built up and the tail swayed a bit as we hit the mud plain. Mud quickly covered every window, leaving us totally blind to the outside world. With my foot to the floor, the loud engine whined—but suddenly all movement ceased. I hit the gas again, only to have the tires continue to spin, shooting up mud in all directions but with no forward progress.

It became obvious that we were stuck. To assess the situation I tried to get out to look around, but the doors would not open. "That's funny . . . Can you guys open your doors?" I asked the rest of the crew. They were having the same problem. Finally with some pushing I was able to open a door, shoving aside a thick brown pile of mud in the process. We had sunk in mud all the way past the doorjambs.

What a mess! There we were, literally sunk in the middle of a mud plain. I heard the laughs from the far side of the creek as the team witnessed our plight. They quickly returned to see if they could help, and it was then I realized what had happened. The first team had a soft-shelled or canvas-covered Humvee, which was much lighter than ours. The one I was driving was a fully loaded,

If we did not get this thing unstuck, I would be left returning to base, having to inform leadership I sank a Humvee on an Army post.

"up-armored" combat-ready Humvee with bulletproof windows, body armor, and a gun turret for an MK-109 grenade launcher or M-60 machine gun. In my haste to follow the other vehicle's lead across the creek, I failed to consider that I had close to 5,000 pounds of extra weight on my vehicle.

We all got out, slipping around the vehicle and up to our knees in mud, assessing the situation. We deployed the winch from the front of the Humvee, trying multiple configurations to no avail. Daylight was fading, and if we did not get this thing unstuck, I would be left returning to base, having to inform leadership I sank a Humvee on an Army post and was unable to retrieve it. Needless to say, this is not what a lieutenant wants to tell his commander. And that commander wants no part of calling the general, letting him know they will need some help from their Army counterparts to rescue a sunken Humvee.

The team huddled around a huge oak tree, assessing the options. Someone offered, "Hey, can't we get an M-Series Wrecker back here to get us out?" The M-Series Wrecker could get anything out, as it was designed to drag tanks out of the mud if need be, but that hulking vehicle would never be able to get back to this remote part of the base and navigate down the ravines on the trail to our location. That wasn't an option. We were either getting this out on our own or it was going to stay here for a while, and I would be looking at some very difficult conversations and maybe even an Article 15 (nonjudicial punishment in the United States Armed Forces) if the vehicle was destroyed and someone felt this had been more of a joyride than a training exercise.

While the group conferred, I walked around back up the ravine a bit to where the senior master sergeant (SMSgt) was standing taking pictures. "I think we are toast. You have any ideas?" I asked him. He had been in the military for almost as long as I had been alive.

Without much hesitation he coolly and unemotionally replied, "Looks like a good training exercise to me. An opportunity for success!" My mind raced with ramifications, consequences, and "what-ifs." We tried to use the winch with the large oak tree off in the distance but the tension on the steel cable around the base of the tree ended up cutting halfway through the tree before we had to stop. We tried anchoring to the other Humvee but we were so stuck that we ended up dragging the Humvee into the mud with us.

The SMSgt and I stood there thinking about our next moves, and that is when he said, "Why not chain one vehicle to the oak tree and then use the winch to see what happens then?" He continued to take pictures.

It was worth a try. I went back to the team and we got everything positioned to give this one last go before the sun went down. We had been digging around the wheels and placing limbs in the tracks to help get some traction. As luck would have it, that, along with the newly positioned support Humvee using its winch, was enough to slowly help our stuck vehicle emerge from the mud. The winch groaned as the engine of the stuck vehicle roared, spitting mud up in the air as the tires finally gained traction and inched the Humvee back to the trail. A loud cheer rang out from the group, and we celebrated with a few high fives while the SMSgt looked on from the crest of the hill, continuing to take pictures. We were covered head to foot in mud, and all the way back to base everyone talked about the ordeal. Most were concerned with where they were going to hose off and what they were going to have for dinner that night. I breathed slowly, knowing I had dodged a bullet, but I still had a lot of work ahead of me. I needed to clean both vehicles before turning them in, and I prayed nothing was wrong with mine. I was also a bit unsure of how the SMSgt would report back to the group commander. And what was up with all the picture-taking? Would I be classified as a reckless young lieutenant?

It took me over an hour back at vehicle operations washing the Humvee, and I knew the guys there would be ticked at all the mud I had left in the racks. It looked like a forest had blown up in there!

The next morning I found a three-ring binder on my desk with page after page of photos of the stuck Humvee and the team working to get it unstuck. The SMSgt had put together a full report calling it a "training exercise" and describing the awesome experience the young lieutenants had on the drop zone, learning about the main mission of the base and the aircrews stationed there. It wasn't long after that I received a call from my squadron commander, and shortly thereafter his boss, the group commander, asking questions. The group commander, a colonel, wanted to let me know the wing commander, a one-star general, had seen the report and wanted me to take him out to the drop zone for a similar tour. Within twenty-four hours, a situation that I thought could have been a career disaster for me turned into a great opportunity where I was getting one-on-one face time with top brass on the base. All this was possible because a seasoned SMSgt saw the situation as an opportunity, not a disaster, and pulled me aside to help me see the situation differently. Once back on base he took matters a step further and promoted the event up the chain of command, highlighting the exercise.

The Logistics Group started a training program for all new lieutenants, mandating they get out to the drop zones and to observe other aspects of the group's work on base, so the lieutenants could experience firsthand all the facets of the operations of the LG (Logistics Group). So not only did I have other base officers wanting to get a similar tour of the drop zone, our unit was soon giving tours to local dignitaries, politicians, and congressmen who came to Little Rock Air Force Base. We were able to give many of them a tour of the drop zone, showing them from the ground level what the C-130 aircrews were doing in training as they disgorged various loads out of the back of the aircraft onto the drop zone. This experience opened up another opportunity for me to serve for a time as the Assistant Executive Officer for the Wing Commander, the general who initially asked for a tour after he saw the report.

WHEN A BAD THING IS ACTUALLY A GOOD THING

In my first book, *The Leap: Launching Your Full-Time Career in Our Part-Time Economy*, I interviewed Tom Darden of Cherokee Investment Partners, who gave incredible career advice when he said, "This is central to understand: if something happens and you think it is good or bad, you really don't know. Many times you may perceive something to be bad, like you get fired or lose your job, but in reality it is good for you because it launches you in a new direction. The inverse is also true. Never form an opinion about your current circumstances because it will almost always be wrong." I have found this to be true so often in my career, where I initially looked at situations as bad but they turned out to be major pivot points in my career.

I have seen this with many others for whom the end of one career or the loss of a job was the catalyst that led them to launch a new business or look for work in a different industry that they ended up finding more rewarding. In one of my career pivots, I left the role as CEO of a large leadership training organization in the direct-sales industry. I was tired and burned out, longing for a change of pace with a new challenge and opportunity to leverage my business skills. I also had a great deal of compassion for, and wanted to help, those who were struggling with the fallout of the post-2008 Great Recession. A great opportunity presented itself for me to join the global nonprofit Crown as their president and help the team rebuild an organization that operates in over 108 countries and had helped over 50 million people in its forty-year existence. I came alive at the challenge and felt like my skills and personal goals were in perfect alignment. That opportunity would never have arisen had I not chosen to make my transition and pursue something different.

Sometimes these changes come in our life and are not directed by us. Sometimes we take the initiative and create the change by making the leap to something new. The key to remember is that if you are experiencing what you perceive as a failure in your life right now, I would encourage you to look at it from a different viewpoint. These moments can be an important pivot to a better future. Just like that SMSgt on the drop zone saw the situation differently than me and reframed my thinking, you can reframe any situation you currently find yourself in. Just like leaving one safe and secure job to do something new led me to a better opportunity, if you are in transition, don't look in the rearview mirror focusing on the past, but look to the future with an expectation and anticipation of something better. Regardless of the situation that led you to the point where you are making a pivot, when you are there something magical is about to happen.

Reporter Eric Weiner highlights a fascinating phenomenon in his *Wall Street Journal* article "The Secret of Immigration Genius." He says that history shows the disproportionate success of immigrant refugees when arriving in new countries. Some notable examples are Victor Hugo, Nikolas Tesla, and Albert Einstein, and the technology sector today is full of examples like Sergey Brin, cofounder of Google; Jerry Yang, founder of Yahoo; and Stepan Pachikov, founder of Evernote, to name a few. Studies show that something bigger than simply working hard is involved here. Weiner asks, "What is it about the act of relocating to distant shores—voluntarily or not—that sparks creative genius?"[1] He goes on to explain that research shows it has less to do with a strong work ethic but rather a "schema violation . . . which occurs when our world is turned upside down." The process of our world drastically changing unlocks "cognitive flexibility" and helps us to become hyper-creative. He goes on to say that "many immigrants possess what the psychologist Nigel Barber calls 'oblique perspective.' Uprooted from the familiar, they see the world at an angle, and this fresh perspective enables them to surpass the merely talented. To paraphrase the philosopher Schopenhauer: 'Talent hits a target no one else can hit. Genius hits a target no one else can see.'"[2]

If you have gone through a situation that has totally upended your life, chances are that without realizing it, you are seeing the world "at an angle" and thus have the ability to unleash a creative potential insight that normally would be very hard to tap into. Don't waste these opportunities. You are in your powerful and creative sweet spot. You have clarity and the motivation to take action, where otherwise you may have been too comfortable to notice and too complacent to take action. This is looking at the proverbial glass as half-full, not half-empty. This is your time . . . your chance . . . seize the moment!

HOW TO SHAKE UP YOUR OWN LIFE

Now, if you haven't experienced a radical shake-up in your life recently, but you still feel you need to create a new environment for growth, you can still create the change you seek.

In 2010, my wife and I both knew we needed a change from Flint, Michigan, where I had been CEO and where we had lived for six years. We did not enjoy the "nine months of winter" as we called it and looked forward to a warmer climate. I loved my hometown and the incredible people there but did not want my children growing up with the blight and economic depression that had hung over the city seemingly since I was a boy. With the Great Recession hitting the mid-Michigan area particularly hard, I wanted a different outlook for my family. With all the places we could have relocated to, we chose Knoxville, Tennessee. Brandi and I were both graduates from the University of Tennessee and already had a strong base of friends and network in the area. We both love the energy, knowledge exchange, and youthful vigor of a college town. Nestled in the Smoky Mountains, near the Great Smoky Mountains National Park, the nation's most-visited national park, Knoxville offers all the amenities of a big city but with a small-town feel. It is a great place to raise a family with a low cost of living, no state income tax, and a pro-business and pro-start-up environment, which I needed. Anchored by an excellent educational system, as well as the nearby Oak Ridge National Laboratory, a massive government presence, the Knoxville region has enjoyed the benefits of these two major economic stabilizers amid global turbulence. Additionally, Knoxville is located at the intersection of two of the nation's largest interstates: I-40, which runs from Barstow, California, to Wilmington, North Carolina, and I-75, which runs from Sault Ste. Marie, Michigan, to Miami, Florida. Getting anywhere on the East Coast is easy and leaves me close to Nashville, Atlanta, Charlotte, Asheville, Chattanooga, and Birmingham.

> **A great way to reinvent yourself is to take the leap and find a perfect area for you and your family and make the move.**

We felt it would be a great place to raise a family and put down some roots. I have met many people who have felt the same way and moved from all over the country to what I think is one of the best-kept secrets on the East Coast.

A recent hire for our company is a young CPA who, with his

wife, left upstate New York to move to Knoxville with no job but with the same goal as me. A great way to reinvent your life or jump-start a new career is to take the leap and find a perfect area for you and your family and make the move. I know many people who have made similar life transitions, moving to Denver, Charlotte, Charleston, Austin, Tucson, and Coeur d'Alene, Idaho.

It isn't just individuals who seek out new locations to make a pivot to start something new; companies employ this strategy too. Boeing moved its headquarters from Seattle to Chicago and in 2016 General Electric's CEO, Jeffrey Immelt, in the middle of a long transformation effort for his company, announced his plan to move the 124-year-old company's headquarters from Connecticut to Boston, citing access to the city's global port, the world's top universities, and its growing technology hub as main reasons.

I know how important a new location can be for a company undergoing a transformation project. For over thirty-five years, Crown had been headquartered in Atlanta. But when I presented our board with the many benefits and cost savings a move to Knoxville could afford, they agreed, and it wasn't long before we officially moved the headquarters there in 2012.

As we've seen, there's nothing like a new environment to help spark significant personal change. Maybe you have not experienced a radical shift in your life that has forced you to see the world differently and has helped unleash your creative power. Possibly you are comfortable (be worried if that is the case), and you know you have been lulled into a sense of security. Perhaps you aren't growing and you realize the world is passing you by. One of the best ways to pivot is to make the leap and be the cause of disruption in your life instead of waiting for it to happen to you. You will be amazed at how your outlook changes when you sit down and start thinking about intentionally designing your life and dreaming of the possibilities. Where do you want to live? What would unlock your fullest potential and make you feel alive again? What do you want to do more than anything else? Where could you have the work/life balance you dream about? You will be surprised at how quickly you will find that sweet spot for yourself, and when you start digging deeper, how many opportunities will start to present themselves. Once again, the hardest part is the first step. The reward is once again dreaming, seeing the world from a new angle, and unlocking potential in you that is lying dormant.

Why are these things important? Many times I speak with people who have lost their jobs, now paralyzed by depression and despair. They see the entire situation as catastrophic. Certainly it is not fun, but I try to help them view the situation from a different perspective in order to see that the situation could be one of the most freeing and liberating times of their lives. They are unencumbered and free to be intentional in crafting the next stage of their life and career! I speak with many who are miserable with their job and unhappy with where they have arrived in life. They followed the career guidance they received in their youth, being promised that certain paths would lead to happiness and fulfillment. Now mid-career, they are left wondering, "Is this as good as it gets? I was not expecting this!" The key is to realize that no matter the situation we all have the power to make a change in our life. It is never too late to get a fresh start. We all have the power to hit the reset button.

MOVING ON FROM LOSS: BEWARE THE THREE P'S

Pivot! You can make a pivot that alters the course of your life. Breaking free from fear and depression is the first step. Sheryl Sandberg, COO of Facebook, unexpectedly lost her husband, Dave Goldberg, in 2015. During a commencement address to the

2016 graduating class of the University of California–Berkeley, Sandberg mentioned the seminal work of Dr. Martin Seligman at the University of Pennsylvania and how it helped her through this time.[3] Dr. Seligman, considered the father of modern positive psychology, developed the "Three P's"—personalization, pervasiveness, and permanence.

These are mindsets we need to free ourselves from as we cope with life's challenges. I highlight Sandberg's story because many of the people I speak with deal with the same issues. She told the graduating class that she had to view her tragedy through the right lens. "Personalization" is what we often tend to do with loss and tragedy. What we need to understand is that things will happen *to* us in life, not necessarily *because* of us. Sheryl wondered if there were things she could have done to help prevent this tragedy. Could her husband's heart problem have been diagnosed? She had to come to the realization that there was nothing she could have done, and sometimes things happen that we can't control.

"Pervasiveness" is the mindset that the challenge or bad thing you're dealing with is all-encompassing. However, says Dr. Seligman, situations are *specific*, not pervasive. Sandberg says that even though she was dealing with immense pain and it felt like her world was crumbling around her, she was able to retreat into her Facebook job and get lost in her work. She realized that, although she was going through a lot, other aspects of her life were okay.

"Permanence" has to do with the (mistaken) idea that something will never change. Sandberg realized that the grief she faced daily with the loss of her husband was terrible, but that it would not be permanent. Things would get better—eventually.

You may experience loss of a job or other career upheavals. Remind yourself that these losses, these failures, are not personal, not pervasive, and not permanent. I work with my children to understand that if they fail a test it doesn't mean they are not smart. It just means they failed a test, and they can regroup, learn that material, and get an A on the next test. Winston Churchill said it best when he said, "Success is not final. Failure is not fatal."[4]

SEEING WORK DIFFERENTLY

The second step is to understand the larger picture. Once we are free from limitations of the past and are dreaming about the future, we can ask, "Is it possible to have a restorative career? A career where I feel whole, empowered, fulfilled, and where I know I am making a difference in the world?" That is the most powerful question. When we start to look at work differently, it will lead us down an entirely different path leading to better results.

If I were to buy back time, how would I use it?

For most of my career I viewed work as a transaction. I was taught that every worker was equal to a monetary value (per hour), based on the value of work we could perform or produce. This is a basic tenet in economics, one that we learn from an early age. If we don't want to earn minimum wage, we are told to go to college, earn a great degree, and go work in a higher-paying career field, where we can produce higher-valued work and command a higher wage.

This is a relatively simple economic equation that everyone knows. This transactional system is set up where we trade time for money. Better said, we give our life for a monetary value based on the value we produce. We need to understand the opportunity cost in everything that we do in life.

I wonder, if I were on my deathbed, how much would I be willing to pay to buy back a few hours, days, weeks, months, or even years of my life, if that were possible? Staring into eternity with moments left to live, what will be my final thoughts? Will I have any regrets? If I could buy back time, how would I use it? Would it give me the opportunity to do things I wish I had done? Would it allow me to love and say things to people I wished I had said? Could I serve more people? Could I have a greater impact? Did my life matter in the balance of eternity?

Looking at work from a transactional standpoint cheapens us. It cheapens those with whom we work. Our value is far greater than the economic equivalents on file in the HR department. The government has stepped in to protect the people to ensure a fair minimum wage. Today it stands at $7.25 per hour, but when I think about it that just seems grotesque to think of buying an hour of a person's life for $7.25. When you see this transaction system for what it is, it allows us to view things differently. Even top attorneys or other professionals who are able to command $400 to $600 per hour for their time based on knowledge and skill seem to be inadequately valued when you think that those "billable hours" are part of a person's life!

However, we were not designed to be transactions, and we should not view ourselves and others solely through that lens. Our work is part of a restorative process for us, for others, and for the entire world. If you believe that we all have been created by a God who loves us and designed each of us uniquely with a special purpose, we are empowered and unleashed to do good in the world.

You and I serve a higher purpose. Our lives are not bought but we give them, invest them, and willingly spend them doing what we have been gifted by God to do. We should never view ourselves and others based solely on some economic value to determine our societal worth. It is easy to do as people compare yearly salaries and hourly rates, but this is not the sum total of human worth. Human life and our worth is measured much differently by God.

When we have a proper understanding of the theology of work, we understand these three things:

Work is part of our worship of God—In all we do, we seek to glorify and honor Him from the most important task to the least. Our call is to be faithful in the execution of our duties, no matter the circumstances.

Work is part of our relationship with God—Just as He gave Adam a job in the garden of Eden, we all have been given a job here on earth. Each one of us has a special role to play and those who are found faithful will be given more.

Work is part of our relationship with others—Whether we steward the reins of a big business employing others or are working for ourselves, our work is part of our relationship to bless others. Remember the Parable of the Vineyard owner and the story of Joseph? Like Joseph, we need to be faithful and realize our work is not just to support us but also for the good of society and to help others. Jesus gave the commandment to love our neighbor, and our work is a practical way to do that. Remember the story of the Good Samaritan.

When we understand these three simple but powerful points, we can never look at work the same way again. We can never view others in the same old economic equation. There is no economic hierarchy in God's eyes. He is concerned with our faithfulness. We are all equal, and He requires us to steward the gifts and talents He has placed in us, as well as the positions He has placed us in. He requires that we help the poor and treat people fairly, and that we faithfully perform the responsibilities He has called us to.

When we understand this truth, it inspires us to seek out God's calling in our lives and to make sure we have not made any mistake by simply doing what we want but rather are performing the work that God has designed and destined us to do.

This attitude allows us to escape the negative influence of the transactional model. When we buy into this model and accept that our only value is defined by our worth, X per hour, we are trading our very lives for money. In this tragedy, the natural tendency is for everyone to seek to do the least amount of work or expend the least amount of energy possible, while maximizing the reward or pay as much as possible.

From a micro-perspective this is damaging for a person's self-perception, attitude, and career as over time it hinders influence and quality work. From a macro-perspective, it hurts the business and overall greater economy. We have been called to so much more. As a Christian I believe that I represent Christ in all I do and should never give less than my best in any endeavor.

We believe that we each have a God-given design and role to play, and that we have the power to intentionally design our lives to accomplish that purpose. Any disappointment along the way can be seen as a catalyst to help us pivot to where we should be. Instead of being fearful and depressed, we can have a positive outlook, focusing on our future goals and taking steps to get there. These hard times develop and hone us. They build character and give us stories to share with those who will be following behind us. Most importantly, these times give birth to our greatest victories.

➤ PIVOT POINTS Owning It

I have learned that the quality of our lives is often determined by the quality of the questions we ask. Asking the right question leads to the right answer. And I was always taught that we learn more from our failures than our victories.

But to do that, it is important to own our failures. We need to know what we did wrong, how we made a bad decision or mistake, and what we can do in the future not to repeat it.

Many people want to gloss over failure, sweeping it into the past as quickly as possible. We don't want to dwell on things but if we don't take the opportunity to own it and then learn from it we are missing a great opportunity for growth and development.

I have never met a mature, wise, and thriving person who didn't own their mistakes. Those who have the professional-victim mentality are those who are masters of never accepting responsibility and blaming others. They never go far in life. Therefore, our next action step is to do the following:

1. What are your biggest life and career failures? Write them down in a journal.
2. What did you learn from them? Write it down.
3. How is your life better today because of those mistakes/failures?
4. From now on, when remembering those moments in your life, make a commitment to only think about what you learned and the ways your life is better because of them. (No more negative thoughts from past failures!) If you have learned from them, they aren't failures anymore, are they? They're opportunities for growth. God always works things out for good.

THE LONG GEAR: SMALL STEPS TO SUCCESS

"I'm a slow walker but I never walk back."
ABRAHAM LINCOLN

Standing in the parking lot of Mt. Rainier National Park in Washington State, I adjusted my seventy-pound backpack one last time, trying to ignore the drizzle of rain slowly soaking my outer shell. As members of our team made final preparations, I looked up the trail to Paradise Glacier, where our journey would begin. Over the next seven days we would circumnavigate the most glaciated peak in North America, conducting a Himalayan seminar to learn all the aspects of Himalayan mountain climbing, with our final goal to reach the summit of Mt. Rainier's 14,417-foot peak. Although not extremely high, this climb up glaciers, over ice fields and deep crevasses, while sleeping on exposed ice shelves, would prove to be a challenge. Our guide reminded us that some of the worst mountaineering accidents in North America had happened on this site, and the goal was not to summit but to get back to the parking lot alive. No risks would be taken to achieve the summit that would put that ultimate goal at risk. I agreed, but I still desperately wanted to reach the peak.

Now I peered up to get a glimpse of it hidden behind the clouds. It seemed so far away, and the thought of standing on the peak seemed impossible. I had to carry seventy pounds of gear for the next seven days, on a climb where each step closer to the peak became tougher as the oxygen levels dropped.

As we climbed, the dangers increased and obstacles were everywhere. Within days, two members of our party had to be evacuated off the mountain due to injury and cold. The slow drizzle turned to snow, and a constant state of cold permeated every fiber of my body. I quickly learned that a long day would get downright miserable if I focused on every pain point and discomfort along the way. The team knew the goal and we had charted our path. After that, the most important discipline was to intentionally *not* look at the summit but focus on the next step in the journey. One step at a time, our boots fixed with crampons, tied to the person in front of us and ice axes in hand, we stepped in unison, took two breaths, and stepped again.

The slow, methodical approach was at first tedious for a track guy who had lived his life running. My mindset was to go fast. Everything was a race, and this slow process was mind-numbing for me. I soon learned that not only was this the safest way to navigate ice fields and deep crevasses, and test the snow-covered glaciers for hidden caverns that could swallow us up with a wrong step, but it allowed me to focus and think as I had never done before. I became intensely present in the moment. No longer thinking of anything but the next step in front of me, I started to develop what we called "the long gear." Like a cyclist on a long-distance ride who shifts into a steady gear and keeps a metronome cadence, allowing him to conserve energy for the duration of the ride, our team developed a long gear for our climb to the summit. The initial discomfort was soon viewed through a new lens of accomplishment as we learned to relish the slow, methodical pace.

The long, slow process allowed for quiet times of introspection and thoughtful analysis of life as we climbed together. Mt. Rainier was a spiritual experience for me, and it came at a pivotal point in my life when I was considering making a huge career leap. My time on the mountain gave me clarity and helped me see my life differently. Away from the noise of the everyday, I used the time to do some soul-searching as I sat under the dark night sky. I pondered and prayed while cold winds whistled as they blew up the glaciers and the stars exploded in the sky above as I had never experienced them before. I tell people that if you want a life-changing experience, go climb a mountain, because I believe it provides an opportunity to see and experience life from a different perspective. Every single one of my climbing partners, on all the journeys I have been a part of, has come away with a similar story.

The morning I reached the summit of Rainier, I signed a log at the top, dedicating the journey to my wife and children and to a close Air Force friend who had recently died of cancer and had inspired me to bust out of my routine and tackle an adventure. Everyone needs a Mike Mann in their life, a person who inspires them to try something difficult and to set high goals. "The long gear" became a term I started to use regularly. Family and coworkers immediately knew what I was referencing when I said we needed to find our long gear on a particular project. After setting a goal, I understood the power of slow, methodical plodding, putting fears and distractions out of my mind to focus on the next step in the process. Although the summits of life might seem too far away, with daily, consistent plodding we would soon be standing on the peak, having accomplished the goal.

NOW TO KILIMANJARO!

The climbing bug bit me hard, and it wasn't long before I was off with friends to climb Mt. Kilimanjaro in Tanzania, Africa. One of the famed Seven Summits and the highest point in Africa at 19,420 feet, the climb wasn't nearly as technical as Mt. Rainier, but the altitude and weather could still present problems. The journey to the summit was one adventure after the next. The summit loomed large in the background as we hiked through rain forests, cactus-filled, desert-like valleys, and multiple temperature zones. As we traversed every ecosystem on earth, the "long gear" was once again in play as we inched closer to the summit and the air grew thin and each day our breathing became more labored the closer we got to our goal. As in life, I learned ease and comfort are the furthest from my goals, and to achieve the things that I truly desire requires the ability to endure long periods of pain and discomfort. It is true that the night is darkest just before dawn.

In a race, I found that the most pain was endured in the final parts of the race as my body battled exhaustion seconds before I crossed the finish line. Mountain climbing is no different.

The morning we set out to summit Kili, we started at 1:00 a.m. from our base camp at 15,000 feet. The long, slow journey to the summit would take us through some of the steepest and toughest climbing on the mountain. If we were lucky we would get to the summit by sunrise and have some time for pictures before the long journey back to camp. Along the way we passed people who had quit because it was too cold and windy and they were having a hard time with the altitude. After hours of watching the light from my headlamp dance on the rocks at my feet and the back of the guy in front of me as the cold wind buffeted the mountain, drowning out any conversation anyone tried to have, I had become frustrated with the snail's pace of the group. The guy behind me was feeling the same way as he kept stepping on my boots, while I bumped into the climber in front of me.

About forty-five minutes from the summit as the group rested, we decided to go ahead alone. The long, slow gear had gotten us this far, but we decided that we would try to pick up the pace and hit the peak before the rest of the group. Confident in my athletic background and training and not having experienced any altitude sickness to this point, I felt I could move faster, and as I had spent the last six hours following in someone's footsteps, I needed a change of pace and scenery. We took off at an aggressive clip. Another group had been climbing with us that morning and was a bit farther ahead of us on the trail, and we quickly caught them and passed them with little trouble. As the sun started to rise in the distance, the mountain awoke and became visible, and we saw the summit just minutes from where we were. I looked back over my shoulder to see two groups of climbers well behind us on the trail, slowly making their way up. I turned to look at the summit and started to climb once again, and it hit me like a lightning bolt. It felt like I had been shot. A sharp pain radiated through my head—the worst pain I had ever experienced. The closest thing I could compare it to was what I imagined it felt like to be shot in the head. Each step became more painful, and I realized I had exerted myself so much in the previous hour, climbing faster than the prescribed rate and much faster than the "long gear," that my body was deprived of oxygen and I was experiencing altitude sickness. I reached the summit and lay down on the ground, waiting for the group below to reach us. We had our moment of celebration together, taking pictures and high-fiving each other on the accomplishment. But I could not hide the pain from the group, and after some rest, water, and pain relievers, I knew I had to get back to base camp as fast as possible. The "peak" moment that should have been a joyous occasion was cut short.

The descent that followed was one of the most physically painful experiences of my life as I struggled down the mountain. Hours later, once we reached our camp, I collapsed in my tent, never removing my boots or clothes, and fell asleep, missing dinner that night. I slept until the next day, only to be awakened by the camp being taken down and members of the team moving out down the mountain. In this case, faster had not been better. Ditching the safe and proven climbing methods, not using the long-gear approach, I tried to take matters into my own hands and sped up to reach the summit faster. I hit the summit first with my climbing partner, but I paid the price physically. Going fast in a track race is great. Racing up a mountain is not great. Or smart.

Sometimes the next step is just reminding ourselves not to quit!

It is always important to know your pace in racing, climbing mountains, and in your career. It is important to know the environment we are performing in and to tailor our methods to achieve our desired goals. We need to understand that our summit (our goal) may seem far off in the distance and almost impossible from where we are currently, but by adopting the long-gear approach of focusing solely on the next step in the journey, soon, without realizing it, we will have traveled a great distance, standing on the summit, having achieved our desired results. Sometimes the next step is just reminding ourselves not to quit!

In the end, it is not just about attaining that goal and standing on that summit, but also savoring the accomplishment. It is possible to achieve our goals without fully enjoying them. I accomplished my goal of reaching the summit of Kilimanjaro, but at the cost of not being able to enjoy it fully with my team. I was in so much pain that the entire day was spent trying to get down that mountain as fast as possible. That is the thing that is etched in my mind forever.

WHAT MAKES A PERSON "SUCCESSFUL"?

As you think about your career goals and dreams and start working with your mentor and coaches to help you accomplish them, remember: don't be so focused on reaching those goals that you forget about the bigger picture. Ask yourself, "What are you willing to pay to accomplish that goal?" I know some people who have set goals in life and were willing to sacrifice everything for those goals. I have seen people sacrifice their health, family, relationships, marriages, integrity, and reputations in the pursuit of a goal. Know what you are willing and not willing to pay for your goals.

As we start to make plans and take action to pivot in our careers, we need inspiration and encouragement to get us moving on the journey. But in addition to encouragement, we need someone to rein us in when necessary, as I found out on Kilimanjaro. Being headstrong and focused to accomplish a goal at all costs has destroyed many lives.

I wish I could tell the cautionary tales I have heard over the years. From fathers who put a pile of cash in front of a young son, telling him, "This is the most important thing in life . . . even more important than you," to those who build great careers, showered with accolades, but have no relationship with their children, to those who ditch a spouse when their career takes off because their life aspirations are now different—success at all costs is not success in my book.

Author Tim Ferriss often asks guests on his podcast to name the first person they think of when they hear the word "successful." The usual names often come up like Bill Gates, Steve Jobs, and others. Many times it is because they have achieved massive success in a very public way, as Bill Gates or Steve Jobs have done. However, from time to time guests mention other names and let the listening audience know that they admire these people for being successful in different ways, for being true to their beliefs, and for making an impact on society and mankind. For me, I want to take a holistic look at a person's life. I am interested in emulating a person who has led a well-balanced life, who has been successful in their career, in their family and personal relationships, and in the larger sphere of trying to make the world a little better.

Those who live life with generosity, aspiring to help others and make a difference, are far more often the types of heroes that captivate the attention of the world at large. Those who give their lives in the service of others are respected in every culture and society. I highly recommend giving this some thought as you start to craft your life plan. Find that person and study the foundations they set in their life and the decisions they made to achieve success. If you are blessed to live a long life and have the ability to look back on your decisions and pivots you made along the way, I am sure that you will be glad you invested the time to understand the secret of their success.

GET BACK UP!

Arguably one of the greatest movie speeches of all time is from the 2006 movie *Rocky Balboa* when Sylvester Stallone, as Rocky, gives his son a speech about life, getting hit and getting back up, never quitting; and never pointing the finger at someone else or at setbacks, but instead continuing to press forward in the face of all adversity. If you have never seen this, I strongly encourage you to check it out. (You can watch the clip at https://www.youtube.com/watch?v=D_Vg4uyYwEk). This clip has been viewed by millions of people, from those attending motivational seminars looking to reinvent their life to high school students in locker rooms preparing to take the field. The short vignette obviously was written by someone who knows firsthand how tough life can be and how to "get back up" when you take a hit.

Nashville, the country music capital of the world, is known as a town where aspiring stars come to shine and hopefully get noticed. For those who travel there, you can venture down to Broadway on any night and find a street full of restaurants and bars playing live music of up-and-coming musicians working hard to get noticed. Their dream is to hone their craft in these venues, playing in front of small crowds, hoping to eventually get discovered like Garth Brooks, Taylor Swift, Keith Urban, Kenny Chesney, and many others did in these same establishments.

I was attending an Agile Development training seminar in Nashville with some friends, and one night we all decided to get dinner on Broadway and listen to some live music. As we walked down the street, a patron let us know the next band was getting ready to play at an establishment and we walked in excited to hear some great music. The crowd was small and eventually became restless as the band continued to mic-check and sound-check all of their equipment. It was obvious that something was wrong with the lead singer's guitar, and he visibly became more and more agitated with the situation. Ten minutes turned to twenty and they issued an apology for the delay and started to play.

We were excited. The music filled the venue with some of our favorite country songs, and people started to sing along. The band members gave it 100 percent, but the lead singer continued to struggle, singing briefly and then fiddling with his guitar and talking with stagehands. His team continued in his absence, playing to the best of their ability, trying to compensate for his distraction. Suddenly he just jumped down from the stage into the audience and walked past everyone, upset and shaking his head, and headed out the back door.

Something in me would not allow this to happen. I had just invested close to forty minutes waiting for them to play, and watching him quit like that on us, the audience, made me mad. I ran after him. By the time I caught him he was out on the street, speaking with a member of the staff and hailing a cab. I overheard him complaining about his amplifier not working, so apparently he was not working either and going home. I grabbed his arm and asked, "Hey, what are you doing?" He was stunned and started to mutter some lame excuse about the amp not working. "So what?" I responded. "Your mic is working and your band is still in there playing. Don't quit! Get back in there and sing! Come on, man! Don't go out like that. Get back in there and put that cord in your guitar and play it like never before. You want it . . . the band wants it . . . and the crowd wants it! It's all about the comeback, dude! It's all about the comeback!"

Without knowing it I was giving him the speech I had been given multiple times before in my life. For some reason that night I was able to pay it forward, encouraging him to not quit but stage an epic comeback. And an epic comeback it was! He was obviously shocked that a member of the audience would follow him outside and get in his face and not let him quit. To our surprise he went back in, jumped back onstage, and started to sing. Moments later house staff from the back brought out a new amp and plugged his guitar in, and HE CRUSHED IT! The next forty-five minutes that band nailed every song, and the small crowd who had stuck around were given a top-notch performance. We all sang and clapped and had a great time.

Life is all about the art of the comeback! We all will need someone to give us this speech at some point and we will need to give it to others to pay it forward. This night was a lesson for me that I have used with others. It reminded me how close the musician was to his summit but quit when things got tough. Without some encouragement he would have been driving home, missing out on a great opportunity—but with some much-needed support he was able to rebound and have success.

Our words have power. I was able to instantly see how a kind word of encouragement helped that guy that evening, but many times we will not be able to see the result so clearly. Yet our words of support and affirmation do make a difference. And we all will need this in our careers. That musician and his team were "journeymen" trying to make it in Nashville. For him to become a star like the ones discovered on Broadway before him, he will need to learn never to quit and to keep going and give 100 percent, even when things aren't working. That is when a star is born. I hope those are lessons he and his team learned that night. If so, they have a chance to make it to the top!

If you and I are honest, we have probably been in similar situations in life, times we walked offstage instead of playing on. I have been there. I've quit and regretted it. I have also experienced moments when I wanted to quit and someone stepped in to encourage me, have faith in me, speak words of life to me, and it made all the difference. I have persevered through some very tough moments to see victory on the other side and am so glad that I had people who encouraged me along the way to help me stay the course.

There will always be an easy exit for each of us, an excuse, something that we can do to temporarily take us out of that uncomfortable environment—but that path will never lead to success.

All of us will have to pivot in our careers, and sometimes we will have to endure periods of frustration and stress. Whether you are a young millennial entering your career expecting to pivot every three or four years like your peers, or you are a baby boomer making a career pivot late in your career out of necessity, we all will be making pivots together in the days ahead. With the constant state of change in our global economy and advancement of technologies that are remaking every industry, we will all find ourselves needing to Revector, Repurpose, Renew, and Reinvent ourselves in our careers.

THE JOURNEY BEGINS WITH A SINGLE STEP

In chapter 1 we looked at the 4 Career Pivots diagram to get a better understanding of the type of pivot we currently need to make based on where we are in our careers. Each one requires a slightly different action plan. To get started putting this together, we need to understand where our greatest opportunity may be. Most people will find their greatest opportunity at the intersection of their current skills, personality type, and past experiences.

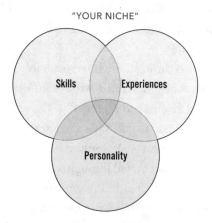

"YOUR NICHE"

Skills · Experiences · Personality

You can't change your past experiences, but you can change how you view them and how you tell your story. You can't change your personality, but you can change by playing to your personality strengths. You can change your skills, making sure you are a lifelong learner adding skills that are critical in the new economy. Only you can set your goals and take the required steps needed to achieve them. My father taught me early in life that the harder you work the luckier you get, and I have found this to be true in my career. Those who wait for a lucky break always get passed by those who are creating their own luck by hard work and staying focused on their goals. Most importantly, never quit!

Going through this exercise is extremely important. Many times people stuck in a bad job or miserable career will get desperate over time and begin to have the philosophy of "anywhere but here!" This can be dangerous as people many times make leaps into situations that end up being no better or even worse than their current situation, all because of their haste for change. Taking time on the front end of your transition to have a deep understanding of your goals, and then to develop an action plan to get there, will greatly improve your transition and opportunity of advancement.

This is not an exercise most people can do alone. We become so myopic in the way we view the world and the situations that we are in that it is imperative we have trusted advisors that we can talk with, sharing our hopes and dreams, our disappointments and frustrations, and to hear their insight. Those who listen to us will pick up on subtle clues that many times we will miss. Our subconscious will be screaming out and many times we miss it due to the noise of life, but those outside of that noise can many times see things clearly that we cannot.

This process will take some time, and I recommend using a coach or mentor to help you evaluate how you analyze these three areas. Using the *Life Plan: Success Guide* from my website, take some time to write down all your experiences, skills, and your personality type after taking a Career Direct Assessment or Personality ID Assessment. Your coach and mentor can help you through the process looking over your résumé and asking more in-depth questions to draw out things you may have missed. I have gone through this process myself. I was updating my CV a number of years ago and asked a friend who was also an executive placement coach to review it to see what he thought. He responded, saying, "Bob, I think you left out some critical things from your past. You don't mention this, you undervalue that, and these things I see that are a huge value in who you are, aren't even included."

I was shocked at how accurate he was. As an outsider he saw things in my career and skills that I had totally missed. With his help I was able to update my CV to reflect those attributes. I have done this enough to know that everyone misses something because over time we all become myopic in the way we view ourselves and backgrounds, experiences, and skills. This is why having someone to help us through this exercise is so important. They give a fresh perspective and draw out things that we miss. This is why I always encourage people to get a one-on-one consultation with a personal coach using the Career Direct assessment.

Experiences

When analyzing experiences, the first thing we can do is to put down in chronological order all of our jobs and positions we have held. For those who have been in their career for a while, it might show a trend line within the same company or industry progressing along a standard career path. We call this a linear career. There will be others who have a diverse background with a wide variety of experiences, having worked in different industries and where no logical career path seems to be forming. This is typical of a non-linear career. But even within the nonlinear career paths of many individuals we can find certain trends. For example, have you also been in leadership positions or have you worked your way into leadership positions over time? These are indicators that we want to highlight in your area of expertise.

Our experiences go beyond just our work lives, however. We want to put down all nonprofit and community work we have been a part of where we have worked with teams and on projects. Social clubs and groups also need to make this list. What networking events and conferences have you attended? As we peel back the layers of the onion, you will start to glean the connection points and data from each. All of this needs to be written down so you can view it and make notes. You will notice over time that you will remember things, and this document will continue to grow as your mentor/coach helps you through the process.

Whether you have a linear or nonlinear career path, there is always a story. It is your job to be able to connect the dots and share that narrative and story with those looking to hire you. What were the reasons you took those jobs? What did you learn? What did you love and dislike about each? How did each job help you progress to the next level in your career? What were your successes and accomplishments? More importantly, what were your failures and disappointments, and what did you learn from them? Many people don't want to talk about failure, and I think this is a big mistake.

No one wants to have a team member who gets weak in the knees when the lifting becomes heavy.

In Silicon Valley, many venture capitalists (VCs) who invest in start-up companies will not invest in young entrepreneurs who have not experienced failure. Failure is part of the learning process, as we have discussed, and those who have failed learn from the experience, becoming stronger and wiser. Investors wonder about people who have never failed and how they will respond when they do. No one wants to have a team member who gets weak in the knees when the lifting becomes heavy.

Don't be embarrassed about failure. Don't try to hide it. Past mistakes or failures are tuition you have paid in life. Own it and know what you learned from it and be able to share it as an experience that has crafted you into the man or woman that you are today. That part of your narrative could be the most important part of your career story to those who are looking to hire you.

Skills

The process for skills is similar. Here we will start with our educational background. We want to list every place we have obtained educational credits, and any degrees or certifications we have earned. If we have taken MOOCs, Nanodegrees, part-time classes, learned trades, or done any other coursework or training, everything needs to be listed here.

Over time we can develop certain types of skills like public speaking, writing, carpentry, various software programs, electrical work, etc. All skills, even the ones that don't come with a degree or certification, need to be listed. This is one of the most important areas for a mentor/coach to help you. We all acquire certain skills in our lifetime, and most of this learning is done after our secondary and postsecondary educations. This is an area where most people will undervalue and leave out important parts of their background. As you are putting this together and sense that you have not updated your skill sets since high school or college, develop an action plan to start acquiring new skills. In a relatively short amount of time by taking a couple of MOOCs, you can obtain new skills that are critical in the new global economy.

Younger people who are digital natives many times will discount their level of experience and understanding in social media platforms and emerging technologies. Companies in every industry are desperate to understand how to engage with the millennial market and how to leverage these new platforms. Understanding how to connect the dots and to show businesses how they can leverage these tools for communication, engagement, marketing, and brand building is important. Many millennials are getting their foot in the door at companies by showing how to leverage these tools. For those who are older (the baby boomer crowd), it is equally important to be well versed in the technology of the day. I have had numerous meetings over the years with people interviewing for a position or pitching a program for my company to implement, and in the course of dialogue when a team member brings up a common technology platform that is ubiquitous in industry and the person has no idea about it or says, "I don't understand that stuff," it is an instant red flag. I have seen meetings basically get shut down right then and there. I immediately know what is going on in the mind of my team member sitting across from me. They are rolling their eyes thinking, "You have to be kidding me! Who is this and where have they been? If they can't use X, there is no way we can work with them."

Here are the key tools that all baby boomers should have accounts on and be able to use. Imagine a secretary forty years ago coming into your office and saying they did not know how to use a typewriter. If you don't have an account on these platforms and know how to use them in the course of business, people will think the same of you today.

1. All Google products. Have a Gmail account; understand how to use Google Drive; become proficient in using Google Hangouts for virtual meetings.
2. Basecamp.com/Trello.com—cloud project management and communication
3. DropBox.com—cloud document storage
4. Skype.com—videoconferencing
5. Zoom.com—videoconferencing

These are the basics. It's like coming to work with pants on. It is just assumed everyone understands these tools and can use them. If you really want to impress folks, let them know you use the following:

6. Slack.com—online team communication, replacing email
7. Evernote.com—cloud notes and document storage
8. Venmo.com—mobile app for payments

I was recently having a meeting with a gentleman who had spent forty years as a technologist, working for big companies around the country, helping them with billion-dollar projects. He had an impressive résumé, but I was unsure what to expect. He had been out of the industry for a while and was doing some consulting, and a lot has changed over forty years. I was wondering if he was going to tell me about some horse-and-buggy technology he used to work on or if he was up to date and in the flow with current trends impacting the world today. He walked in the office and after the small talk sat down at the table with our team and pulled out his Apple iPad and laptop and started to get set up, when I noticed an Apple Watch on his wrist. I was stunned. He was the oldest person I had ever seen wearing an Apple Watch, and it instantly made an impression on me. Within minutes of our discussion it was obvious he was VERY much in the flow with current technologies and was dialoguing deeply with our young millennial programmers and staff on many topics, basically downloading years of knowledge as everyone took notes and hung onto his every word. At the end of the day I told him I was wondering how the day would go, but when I saw his Apple Watch I was immediately impressed. He laughed and told me that he and his partner were sitting in a Starbucks working a few weeks prior, and they had their iPads and iPhones out. Some young guy walked up, leaned over, and said, "Wow! I am so proud of you guys. You know how to use an iPhone and iPad, and you have an Apple Watch too!" As the consultant told me this story, he raised his voice, imitating the young guy making sure the old duffers could hear him. My friend laughed. "I told him, 'Son, my generation invented this stuff. I am glad you know how to use it!'"

I love that moxie. It was motivation for me to continue to learn and pick up new skills and understand new technologies that I don't currently know how to use. If you are mid- to late-career, a baby boomer or older person making a pivot, be that guy! Understanding these technologies are skills that are mandatory in today's economy and anyone with a little time and practice can learn how to use them and leverage them in business.

Personality

Most employers and hiring agencies today are using personality assessments in the hiring process. Lauren Weber wrote in her *Wall Street Journal* article "Today's Personality Tests Raise the Bar for Job Seekers" that "eight of the top ten private employers now administer pre-hire tests in job applications for some positions . . . companies aren't settling for people with minimum skills; they want applicants that stand out in ability and workplace temperament."[1] Companies are taking their time to find those whom they deem the perfect fit for the role. Many times the right skills take a backseat to finding someone who has the personality and personal skills to work well with others and integrate into the culture of the company.

Personality assessments are also the best way to make sure that you are pivoting to the right career where you will be fulfilled and have success. I was recently having dinner with my Harvard Business School professor Boris Groysberg and discussing the global economy. Boris has young children, and I always ask accomplished individuals who have their finger on the pulse of the global economy and higher education what they are doing to prepare their children for the future. Professor Groysberg's field is company development specializing in staff and culture.

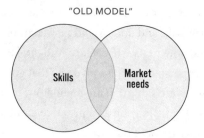

He immediately said the old paradigm was for people to take stock of their skills and see where that intersected the hot markets in the economy. At that intersection is where you would find opportunity. He said the dynamics today have changed, and that there is an equally important question to ask: "What is your passion and purpose?" When you add that to the equation, you now have a Venn diagram that looks like this:

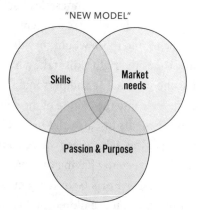

Professor Groysberg said that encouraging his children to understand their purpose in life and to pursue their passions was extremely important for their success in this new economy. Following our passion and purpose unlocks the hidden reservoirs of energy and determination that will be required for us to lock into the "long gear" for the long march to the summit. Don't gloss over this area. It is critical not only for our career success but for our happiness and fulfillment in life.

Those people who have a deep understanding of their personality are a quantum leap ahead of their peers who have no idea and have never taken an assessment before. One of the most in-depth and insightful ones that I have come across that is used globally is Career Direct (www.CareerDirect-GE.org). This assessment gives the user a thirty-three-page report detailing personality, skills, interests, and values. It also shows key industries and career fields where a person with your personality can find a perfect match. Using this report or the condensed four-page version, Personality ID (www.PID.org) can help you in this process. Taking a Career Direct assessment will provide you all the information you need for this section. Without it you will need some help with a trained coach/mentor to really drill down into your personality and how it can impact your career and the right career paths you need to explore based on your personality. For those who will be using career services and will be interviewing for jobs in the future, the Career Direct report will give you a good idea of the types of personality assessments many companies are using in the interview process. I recommend getting comfortable with the process prior to your first interview.

With all the data from these three areas written down in your career journal, you can start to work with your mentor/coach to devise a proper plan for your pivot. For those who are in the Revector, Repurpose, and Renew career quadrants (see graph on p. 66) and currently have a job, your pivot action plan will help you find where you want to be in the future and start building the action steps and plans needed to get there. You need to start taking action today, but you have some time to plan and take baby steps in that direction.

Those who are in the Reinvent career quadrant or those currently without a job are in a different situation. If this is you, you are probably stressed and hurting. I've known a lot of people who have been in this place for an extended period and by the time they start seeking help are ready to take action immediately to alleviate the pain. Those who are unemployed are in a similar situation. You don't have weeks and months to ponder about a career pivot; you need a job today to pay the bills. In this case we are looking at crafting a short-term plan that helps you with current cash flow and obligations, even if it is not your ideal job while you plan and prepare for your big career pivot that will eventually move you into your dream job.

I know how daunting it can be to start the process of trying to take stock of your skills, experiences, and personality, which includes understanding your passion and purpose. During each one of my career pivots I had multiple career coaches and advisors that helped me drill down to the essence of what I was looking for at that time in my life. My mentors helped me see blind spots and to value skills that I was undervaluing at the time. They also helped point me in the right direction to discover opportunity that I was having a hard time seeing on my own. Your Career Direct consultant can do this for you.

CONFESSIONS OF A WORKAHOLIC

My desk is littered with business books, stacks of notes, writing projects, and other things you would expect on an executive's desk, but for my family and those who knew me well from many years ago, conspicuously missing is the large model of a Gulfstream jet that had been a centerpiece for years. It is now replaced with family pictures, children's notes, and drawings. During my last assignment in the Air Force, I was an aide-de-camp to a four-star general, and we traveled the world on a Gulfstream V and a Boeing 737, both painted to look like Air Force One. It was a great assignment and I loved the convenience of private air travel. Once you get accustomed to the ease and flexibility it offers, it is hard to go back to waiting in long lines at the airport, security checks, and cramped seats on those long flights. As I transitioned into the private sector, I was privileged to be able to travel on private business jets often as a perk of my CEO role and had many friends who owned their own planes. It didn't take long for me to set that as a personal goal.

My mother and father taught me to work hard and be the best I could be at whatever I was doing at the time. However, in my early thirties, I became fixated on my own version of success. Like my disastrous climb on Mt. Kilimanjaro, I started sacrificing important things in life in the pursuit of personal success. I took something good, my internal wiring for hard work, and took it to unhealthy extremes. Luckily, with some soul-searching and good mentors, I came to the realization that I needed to change. I needed to completely repurpose my life and career to put what was most important to me—my faith and family—in the center.

My journey eventually led me to Crown, a global nonprofit, which had most of my personal contacts questioning what type of midlife crisis I was suffering to leave the for-profit world for a job that was obviously not on my original career track. As a man of faith, I believe the transition was divinely inspired. It was just what I needed.

Over the past five years my life has been radically altered for the better, allowing me to have times of introspection and rebalancing. This career pivot was life-altering and got me back on track. It is said that once an alcoholic, always an alcoholic. You battle the disease forever. In my case, I have the "workaholic" DNA deep inside of me, and this can be helpful or harmful. I am predisposed to overworking but want to leverage that to be the best I can be—at healthy levels. It requires daily work to stay in balance and mentors in my life to ensure I stay on track. My mindset has changed. I have lofty goals for myself, for my children, and for Crown. However, I have become more mission- and purpose-driven and people-focused, with my ultimate goal to "finish well."

At the end of my life when I stand before God, I want to hear, "Well done, thou good and faithful servant!" To hear that, I know I need to daily stay focused on things that matter, focusing more on others and less on me. I know this life is short. The Bible says it is a fleeting breath, here and then gone. What we do in this life matters for eternity. I know I need to work to repurpose myself and my goals for the larger good of others around me and to make a difference in the world. I know what I am willing to sacrifice and more importantly what I will not sacrifice to attain the goals I have set in my career and in my life.

Have you ever noticed that God rarely uses straight lines in nature? As I travel the world and witness the most amazing scenes, such as the Grand Canyon, Rocky Mountains, Mt. Kilimanjaro, the Serengeti, and the South Pacific island archipelagoes, I can see that the master Architect and Designer uses a system of varied and disordered-appearing tangents with everything—yet it comes together in the most masterful way. So, too, our lives and careers will rarely be linear as we plan. At times we may appear to jump from place to place with the twists and turns of our life not making much sense, but as we look back with the benefit of future insight and perspective we will see a master plan where everything

> **We were all taught that the shortest distance between two points is a straight line. That might be the case in geometry, but it isn't always true in life.**

worked together perfectly. Don't be worried if it appears that you have a nonlinear career. If you do, you are on the right path. We were all taught that the shortest distance between two points is a straight line. That might be the case in geometry, but it isn't always true in life. God has His own plans, and trusting Him is always best and the journey is always rewarding. Work hard and enjoy the journey, being open and willing to move in an unexpected direction as you are called.

As you start your journey I encourage you to ask yourself, what is success to you? It is important to know what your long-term objective is; otherwise the steps we take could pull us in the wrong direction. What are you willing to sacrifice to attain that goal? Many times at seminars and self-help conventions, leaders will talk about being willing to "sacrifice for the dream." It is an important exercise to go through, but I have seen many people who were so focused on their goals and committed to doing whatever it took to achieve them that they unwittingly sacrificed very important things in life and did not realize it until it was too late. If you sacrifice your marriage, family, and children, you can never get that time back, and many times the relationships are forever damaged. Many people will delude themselves by saying, "I am doing this for my family." I was one of those people and it was just a great excuse for me to justify my workaholic ways, putting my goals ahead of the well-being of those closest to me.

To achieve any worthwhile goal in life, we will have to make sacrifices. Sacrifice the things that don't matter, but never sacrifice the things that are most important. I am willing to sacrifice television and *Monday Night Football* and similar diversions to achieve success for my family and company. I won't, however, sacrifice time with my wife and children. Each of us will have different boundaries, and those will change over time. There will be seasons in life when we have to flex in different directions, but as long as we can get back to center that is okay. Know what is most important to you in life, and know what you won't sacrifice! History is replete with warnings about those who would sacrifice the important on the altar of the trivial. It is a struggle that every generation has had to battle. Mark 8:36 says, "What good is it for someone to gain the whole world, yet forfeit their soul?" It is said that the road to ruin is paved with good intentions, and most who end up there certainly did not anticipate their decisions and sacrifices early in their career could create so much damage.

You are about to embark on a journey to pivot in your career with a goal to love your work. Your pivot might be one mentally, or one of slight adjustments, or it could be as massive as moving across the country to start something new. Whatever you do, your decisions as you work through this process will be life-altering. Take time to craft a proper plan and seek wise counsel and advisors who can help you along the way.

It is also very important to have a proper understanding of success. Each individual might define success differently. Everyone will have different goals. However, from a biblical standpoint it is important to remember that God views success as faithfulness. You will be successful in all areas of life if you are faithful. We know that those you are faithful with the little things will be trusted with great things. It has taken me years to refine my version of success away from material possessions, positions and titles, awards and accolades that I sought after in my youth. Chuck Bentley says often that, "The world is not in danger of running out of resources but it is in danger of running out of faithful stewards." My goal is to measure success on being faithful with the what I have been trusted to steward and I hope this will be your goal as well. Success in your job, work, career, and all areas of your life will be based in large part on how faithful you are in the stewardship of your talents and the position and resources you have been given. In the process, you will have true success and will help make the world a better place.

Most importantly, I encourage you to remember that you have one life to live, and that every decision we make has eternal consequences. I have found that when I view my life and decisions through that lens, I am helped to better prioritize and stay focused on what is truly important. I wish you the best in your journey as you seek God's plan for you!

> ## ➤ PIVOT POINTS Crafting Your Plan

Congratulations for all the progress you have made! You have been following the action steps at the end of each chapter and have completed the following.

1. You have built routines to get plugged in to changes in the global economy to understand how it will impact you, and to make pivots before others in your industry.

2. You have taken a Career Direct assessment. You have a better understanding of your wiring and how you have been designed, helping you understand where you will have the greatest opportunity for success.

3. You received a personalized Career Direct consultation and have a subsequent action plan for next steps.

4. You have a list of ways to add new skills, certifications, and Nanodegrees to your résumé, becoming a lifelong learner and helping your chances for future promotions.

5. You developed your résumé and started making contacts with local and national placement services. You also did

the Dickens Process to view your life in the future to tap in to the emotion needed to make life-altering changes that can sometimes be difficult to make.

6. You know your entire story and know how to craft this into a compelling narrative, connecting the dots of how your story seamlessly connects with the companies you wish to work for.

7. You know your biggest life/career failures and what you learned from each of them. You also know how your life is better because of them and you try to only focus on those points as you move forward. Your failures have become opportunities for success because you have learned something in the process from each of them.

Finally, the last action steps require you to write down your goals. When I speak around the country, I encourage audiences to remember the "**GOALS**" as the following:

G = God—Always put God first. God's principles change everything. He loves you and has a plan for you!

O = Others—We are at our happiest and have peace and contentment when we are serving and helping others.

A = Attitude—Attitude is everything! We control it and our response to any situation. Every successful person I have met has had high emotional intelligence and controls their attitude. They always work to have a positive attitude in life.

L = Learning—Becoming a lifelong learner is more critical for our generation than those that preceded us. The pace of change is greater than ever, and continuing to learn and develop is the way to stay ahead.

S = Self—Put yourself last and remember that success comes by putting others first. The Golden Rule continues to hold true today. It is also critical to know yourself! Know who you are, why you are here, and never lose sight of your GOALS.

To get started on your goals, take the work you started in chapter 5 regarding the specifics you are looking for in your career, and craft it into a carefully thought-out game plan for the future. Remember, the more specific, the better. Focus on everything from company culture, job, location, career field/industry, pay, benefits, impact on the world, etc. This will help you know when opportunities come your way if they will meet your goals. Start crafting a plan with your mentor, advisor, or coach with timelines and action items that you need to perform to achieve your desired results.

NOTES

Chapter 1: Here Comes the Tide of Change!

1. Richard Bak, *Henry and Edsel: The Creation of the Ford Empire* (Hoboken, NJ: John Wiley & Sons, 2003), 54–63.

2. "Fisher Body History," http://www.fisherco.com/heritage/.

3. Marjo Johne, "Is a midlife career change a retirement killer?" *The Globe and Mail*, February 9, 2016, http://www.theglobeandmail.com/globe-investor/retirement/retire-lifestyle/a-mid-life-career-change-can-stress-family-finances/article28644731/.

4. American Institute for Economic Research, https://www.aier.org/CCwebform-OWS.

5. Reid Hoffman, Ben Casnocha, and Chris Yeh, *The Alliance* (Boston: Harvard Business Review Press, 2014), 3.

6. Ibid., 3.

7. Marshall Goldsmith and Mark Reiter, *What Got You Here Won't Get You There* (New York: Hyperion, 2007), 212.

8. Neil Irwin, "Aughts were a lost decade for U.S. economy, workers," January 2, 2010, *Washington Post*, http://www.washingtonpost.com/wp-dyn/content/article/2010/01/01/AR2010010101196.html?hpid=topnews.

9. Jonathan Vanian, "Ignore the Internet of Things at Your Own Risk," *Fortune*, November 2, 2015, http://fortune.com/2015/11/02/internet-of-things-irrelevant/.

10. D'Vera Cohn and Paul Taylor, "Baby Boomers Approach 65—Glumly," Pew Research Center, December 20, 2010, http://www.pewresearch.org/daily-number/baby-boomers-retire/.

11. Conner Forrest, "3D printers in space: How the maker movement made it to the final frontier," Tech Republic, July 22, 2016, http://www.techrepublic.com/article/3d-printers-in-space-how-the-maker-movement-made-it-to-the-final-frontier/.

12. Neil Gaiman, Commencement speech at the University of the Arts 2012, https://www.youtube.com/watch?v=ikAb-NYkseI.

13. Jeetu Patel, "Software is still eating the world," Tech Crunch, June 7, 2016, https://techcrunch.com/2016/06/07/software-is-eating-the-world-5-years-later/.

Chapter 2: The Power of Restorative Work

1. Alyson Shontell, "80% Hate Their Jobs—But Should You Choose a Passion or Paycheck?" Business Insider, October 4, 2010, http://www.businessinsider.com/what-do-you-do-when-you-hate-your-job-2010-10.

2. Jerry Bowyer summarizes his interview with Peter Berger in "Is Religion an Essential Driver of Economic Growth?" *Forbes* (May 29, 2013), www.forbes.com/sites/jerrybowyer/2013/05/29/is-religion-an-essential-driver-of-economic-growth/ (accessed May 25, 2015).

Chapter 3: The Four Career Quadrants

1. Julia Greenberg, "Once Upon a Time, Yahoo Was the Most Important Internet Company," *Wired*, November 23, 2015, http://www.wired.com/2015/11/once-upon-a-time-yahoo-was-the-most-important-internet-company/.

2. Keith H. Hammonds, "The Strategy of the Fighter Pilot," *Fast Company*, May 31, 2002, http://www.fastcompany.com/44983/strategy-fighter-pilot.

Chapter 4: Knowing Your Transcending Career Skills

1. Lindsay Gellman, "Stanford's Business School Tells M.B.A.s to Wait on Startups," *The Wall Street Journal*, December 2, 2015, http://www.wsj.com/articles/stanfords-business-school-tells-m-b-a-s-to-wait-on-startups-1449077572.

2. Steve Jurvetson, Draper Fisher, Astro Teller, Christina Smolke, "Forecasting the Future of Technology," eCorner, October 7, 2015, http://ecorner.stanford.edu/videos/3568/Forecasting-the-Future-of-Technology-Entire-Talk.

3. Ibid.

4. President Charles M. Vest, "Leadership in a Technological Age," MIT, June 4, 1999, http://web.mit.edu/president/communications/com99.html.

5. Laszlo Bock, *Work Rules!: Insights from Inside Google That Will Transform How You Live and Lead* (New York: Twelve, 2015), 236–37.

6. *Harvard Business Review*, quoted in Daniel Goleman, "Emotional Intelligence," http://www.danielgoleman.info/topics/emotional-intelligence/.

7. "The 25 Most Influential Business Management Books," *Time* magazine, http://content.time.com/time/specials/packages/completelist/0,29569, 2086680,00.html.

8. Travis Bradberry and Jean Greaves, *The Emotional Intelligence Quick Book* (New York: Simon & Schuster, 2005), 51.

9. Frank Luntz, *Words That Work* (New York: Hyperion, 2007), xvi.

10. Steve Jurvetson, Draper Fisher, Astro Teller, Christina Smolke, "Forecasting the Future of Technology," eCorner, October 7, 2015, http://ecorner.stanford.edu/videos/3568/Forecasting-the-Future-of-Technology-Entire-Talk.

11. Alan Murray, "Four Takeaways From the Fortune Global Forum," *Fortune*, November 12, 2015, http://fortune.com/2015/11/12/takeaways-fortune-global-forum/.

12. Columbia Business School Centennial Dinner, http://www.cultivatingculture.com/wp-content/uploads/2012/10/Henry-Kravis-Accepts-Centennial-Award-copy.pdf.

13. Gary Vaynerchuk, "4 New Year's Resolutions You Should Make to Improve Your Career," GaryVaynerchuk blog, https://www.garyvaynerchuk.com/new-years-resolutions-career/.

14. Katryn Zickuhr and Lee Rainie, "A Snapshot of Reading in America 2013," Pew Research Center, January 16, 2014, http://www.pewresearch.org/fact-tank/2015/10/19/slightly-fewer-americans-are-reading-print-books-new-survey-finds/.

15. Effective Language Learning, http://www.effectivelanguagelearning.com/language-guide/language-difficulty.

16. George Arnett, "Foreign direct investment: which countries get the most?" *The Guardian*, June 24, 2014, https://www.theguardian.com/news/datablog/2014/jun/24/foreign-direct-investment-which-countries-get-the-most.

Chapter 5: Make It Happen

1. TED: Ideas Worth Spreading, "Smash fear, learn anything," by Tim Ferriss, April 2009, https://www.ted.com/talks/tim_ferriss_smash_fear_learn_anything/transcript?language=en.

2. Richard Feloni, "Former Navy SEAL commander explains the philosophy that made his unit the most decorated of the Iraq War," Business Insider, November 10, 2015, http://www.businessinsider.com/retired-navy-seal-explains-why-discipline-is-freedom-2015-11.

3. http://www.npr.org/2011/02/08/133474431/a-successful-job-search-its-all-about-networking.

4. Simon Sinek, "Start with Why," YouTube, https://www.youtube.com/watch?v=sioZd3AxmnE.

Chapter 6: Currents of Growth and Opportunity

1. Kris Lyle, "Should you stay in or get out of academia? Eric Weinstein weighs in," Old School Script, May 16, 2016, http://www.oldschoolscript.com/blog//eric-weinstein-on-staying-in-or-getting-out-of-academia.
2. Tesla Website, https://www.tesla.com/model3.
3. Kashmir Hill, "21 Things I Learned About Bitcoin from Living on It for a Week," *Forbes*, May 9, 2013, http://www.forbes.com/sites/kashmirhill/2013/05/09/25-things-i-learned-about-bitcoin-from-living-on-it-for-a-week/#1519fd3027ca.
4. Don Tapscott, "Blockchain, unblocked: its implication for enterprise computing," ZDNet, July 8, 2016, http://www.zdnet.com/article/blockchain-unblocked-its-implications-for-enterprise-computing/.
5. https://www.engadget.com/2016/08/24/google-hires-satellite-exec-project-loon.
6. "Performance and Capacity Implication for Big Data," IBM, http://www.redbooks.ibm.com/redpapers/pdfs/redp5070.pdf.
7. Thomas Davenport, "Data Scientist: The Sexiest Job of the 21st Century," *Harvard Business Review*, October 2012 issue, https://hbr.org/2012/10/data-scientist-the-sexiest-job-of-the-21st-century/.
8. Ira Wolfe, "65 percent of Today's Students Will Be Employed in Jobs That Don't Exist Yet," Success Performance Solutions, August 26, 2013, http://www.successperformancesolutions.com/2013/65-percent-of-todays-students-will-be-employed-in-jobs-that-dont-exist-yet/.
9. Daniel Pink, *A Whole New Mind* (New York: The Penguin Group, 2006), 154.
10. Ibid.

Chapter 7: Leverage Failure

1. Eric Weiner, "The Secret of Immigrant Genius," *The Wall Street Journal*, January 15, 2016, http://www.wsj.com/articles/the-secret-of-immigrant-genius-1452875951.
2. Ibid.
3. https://www.youtube.com/watch?v=iqm-XEqpayc.
4. http://www.brainyquote.com/quotes/quotes/w/winstonchu124653.html.

Chapter 8: The Long Gear: Small Steps to Success

1. Lauren Weber, "Today's Personality Tests Raise the Bar for Job Seekers," April 14, 2015, http://www.wsj.com/articles/a-personality-test-could-stand-in-the-way-of-your-next-job-1429065001.

RESOURCES AND WEBSITES

Résumé/Portfolio Websites
LinkedIn.com (everyone)
GitHub.com (programmers/coders)
Pathbrite.com (build your online portfolio)

Personal Development Websites
TalentSmart.com
TheMuse.com
PersonalityID.com
CareerDirect—GE.org

Finding a New Job
LinkedIn Jobs
Poacht
Switch
Jobr
Poachable

Indeed
Simply Hired
Glass Door
Internships.com
JobCase.com

Funding for Start-ups or Side Projects
GoFundMe.com
Kickstarter.com
Indiegogo.com

Education/Advancing Skills
EdX.org
KhanAcademy.org
Udacity.com
Coursera.org
GeneralAssemb.ly
ReFactorU.com (Navy SEALs Boot Camp for coders. In-person, eleven-week course, but with amazing results! If you want to be a professional programmer fast, this is the track for you.)

Finding Freelance or Part-Time Work
TaskRabbit.com (only in select cities)
Freelancer.com
ELance.com
Etsy.com
UpWork.com
OnForce.com
TrustedPartner.com

Finances

Crown Money Life Personal Finance Study—(join a ten-week course online at www.Crown.org)

Mint.com (to help you keep track of your finances)

LearnVest.com (to help you start investing)

SoFi.com (refinance your high-interest student loans)

ChristianCreditCounselors.org (help getting out of credit card debt)

Health Care for Self-Employed and Freelancers

FreelancersUnion.org

Books Referenced

Whole New Mind: Why Right-Brainers Will Rule the Future by Daniel Pink

How the Mighty Fall: And Why Some Companies Never Give In by Jim Collins

The Alliance: Managing Talent in the Networked Age by Reid Hoffman, Ben Casnocha, and Chris Yeh

The Influencer Economy: How to Launch Your Idea, Share It with the World, and Thrive in the Digital Age by Ryan Williams

5 Voices: How to Communicate Effectively with Everyone You Lead by Jeremie Kubicek

Emotional Intelligence: Why It Can Matter More than IQ by Daniel Goleman

Primal Leadership: Realizing the Power of Emotional Intelligence by Daniel Goleman, Annie McKee, and Richard E. Boyatzis

The Emotional Intelligence Quick Book by Travis Bradberry and Jean Greaves

Words That Work: It's Not What You Say, It's What People Hear by Frank Luntz

The 4-Hour Work Week: Escape 9-5, Live Anywhere, and Join the New Rich by Tim Ferriss

The Leap: Launching Your Full Time Career in Our Part-Time Economy by Bob Dickie

Work Rules!: Insights from Inside Google That Will Transform How You Live and Lead by Laszlo Bock

ACKNOWLEDGMENTS

This truly has been a family project and I want to thank my wife, Brandi, and our children, Lachlan, Trista, London, Amaris, Charlize, and our new addition, Zevidiah Kingston, for your patience and support as I labored in my spare time to write this book, which took up many weekends and even bled over to our family summer vacation and Christmas break! I won't be writing a book during our next vacation, I promise! Brandi has joked that I spent more time at the University of Tennessee Library writing these last two books than I did when I was a student there! I'd also like to thank Drayton Wade for helping to edit this book and his family for allowing me to put the finishing touches on this book while staying at their *White-A-Morn* family estate in beautiful Beaufort, South Carolina.

I'd also like to thank the Moody staff for their support and encouragement in this process. To my publisher, Randall Payleitner, thank you for continuing to pull and prod and help bring this book to life. To Natalie Mills, who started with the project but made a big career pivot in the middle of it, I thank you for helping us get started in the right direction and I cheer you and your husband on in your new adventure! To my editor, Betsey Newenhuyse, for your amazing attention to detail, thoughts, questions, prodding, and coaching throughout this process to take my mess and make it into the book that it is. I am in your debt! To the extended Moody family, those who have interviewed me on your various radio programs around the country, I greatly appreciate your support.

I would also like to thank my Young Presidents Organization (YPO) classmates in the Harvard Business School Executive Education Program for their encouragement in these projects and for the diverse dialogue on global issues that has helped me refine the way I think of and view the world. The diversity of worldviews and perspectives presented in a safe environment of mutual respect and admiration is the thing I most value in our program. Thank you, Chuck Bentley, for being such a great friend and continually encouraging me to find my voice and speak to the things I am passionate about. I appreciate your mentorship and encouragement. To the Crown family, I love you all and it has been one of the greatest joys in my life to have the honor to serve alongside each of you. Each of you has impacted me and taught me something that has made me a better person. Thank you!

Finally, I would say thank you to *The Leap* and *Love Your Work* launch teams and those who have become supporters of both of these books. I have learned how hard it is to write and market a book and it is impossible without an audience that resonates with the work and shares it with friends and contacts who might be helped by the content. I can't thank you enough! From sending in emails with ideas to helping edit the book, writing reviews on Amazon, and coordinating speaking engagements, you are the best launch team a writer could ask for. Special thanks to the launch team who stepped up and went above and beyond the call of duty to get behind this project. Each of you made an incredible difference and I am forever in your debt. Thank you!

ABOUT THE AUTHOR

Robert Dickie III has served as a decorated Air Force officer, the CEO of an international company, and as the leader of several nonprofits. Since 2011 he has served as president of Crown, a global ministry providing education and training in personal finance, career development, and business management. He holds degrees from the University of Tennessee and the University of Arkansas and is currently participating in the Harvard Business School Executive Education Program, and a member of the Young Presidents Organization. He is the author of *The Leap: Launching Your Full-Time Career in Our Part-Time Economy*. He and his wife, Brandi, have six children.

I WAS HUNGRY

....for a real solution to poverty

> I have mananged to get enough food to feed my family and surplus for another 6 families. I used to work for people who could not pay me. After the training, people are now paying me. **So I Was Hungry, but now I'm fed. I'm now enough!**

TRANSFORMING COMMUNITIES BY TEACHING FAITHFUL STEWARDSHIP OF

Land

Family

Finances

MY WIFE BRANDI AND I have been so moved by seeing how lives are transformed through the I Was Hungry initiative that we are donating profits of this book to this cause. Please join us in bringing hope and practical help to the poorest of the poor in Africa, even the smallest donation will make a difference in lives of the worlds poorest and many times forgotten.

- Bob Dickie

A partnership between Crown Financial Ministries and Foundations For Farming

IWASHUNGRY.NET

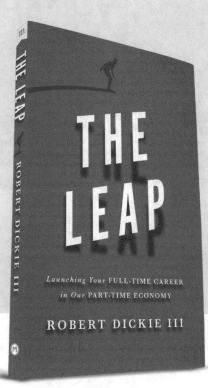

College graduates are facing large student loans and high unemployment rates. Older generations are feeling the effects of the recession as they lose stable jobs and are forced to find new work. The old economy is fading away and a new economy is rising in its place. To succeed in the new economy, we must take a mental leap, rethinking our strategies for success.

MOODYCOLLECTIVE.COM

BRUTAL BOSSES!!! SOUL-CRUSHING CULTURES POISONOUS PEOPLE ➡ THIS BOOK WILL GIVE YOU the CONFIDENCE TO RISE ABOVE THEM ALL.

978-0-8024-0972-0

Insightfully illustrating from real-life stories, *Rising Above a Toxic Workplace* delivers practical hope and guidance for those who find themselves in an unhealthy work environment.

appreciationatwork.com

Also available as an ebook

MOODY
Publishers™

From the Word to Life

Vision Map is a template to start anyone on the path to envisioning and experiencing a God-given dream. God often gives us a difficult problem to solve, and we just need a push in the right direction to find the answer.

Where are you heading?

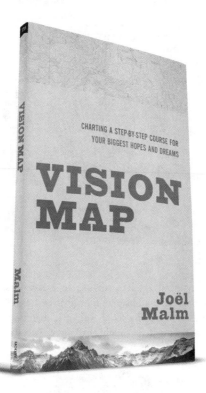

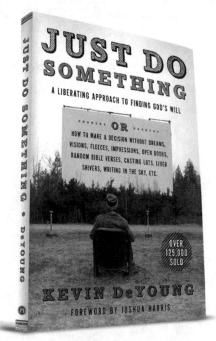

God doesn't need to tell us what to do at each fork in the road. He already revealed His plan for our lives: love Him with our whole hearts, obey His Word, and after that, do what we like. No reason to be directionally challenged. **Just do something.**

MOODY
Publishers™

From the Word to Life

UNLOCK YOUR POTENTIAL
DO MORE. BE MORE.

DISCOVER YOUR UNIQUE DESIGN
AND LEARN HOW TO THRIVE IN IT!

Career Direct is a unique, online assesment designed to help you maximize your God-given talents and abilities. More than a simple career test, four critical areas are analyzed to give you a deeper understanding of how God has wired you.
- Personality
- Interests
- Skills
- Values

Developed over a period of 10 years, and successfully evaluated by more than 150,000+ adults and students worldwide, Career Direct has been tested and validated to help you with both occupational and educational choices.

- Maximize your God-given talents and abilities

- Enjoy job and life satisfaction by choosing the right career field

- Avoid choosing the wrong major

- Available in multiple languages

Perfect for
- Adults
- Students
- Unemployed & misemployed

Career Direct®
Living by Design

www.careerdirect-ge.org

feedback@crown.org